PRAISE FOR
SUPERABOUND

Erin and Steve share a compelling way to break free from limiting beliefs and uninspiring results. If you want to create an extraordinary business and a life that expresses your full potential, I highly recommend *Superabound* to help you on your path.

Dan Sullivan
Co-Founder & President, Strategic Coach®

As I've gotten to know Erin and Steve over the years, I can say that the tools they share in this book are not mere theory. This is the blueprint for how they've created remarkable lives for themselves and helped their clients do the same. *Superabound* is an essential book for anyone who doesn't want to live their life according to someone else's goals but instead to light lanterns on the path to their own vision.

Katrina Ubell, MD
CEO and author of How to Lose Weight for the Last Time

In this excellent book, Erin and Steve show you how to achieve remarkable things and make your dreams a reality. I wish I had the ideas in *Superabound* when I was struggling early in my own career because I would have found my passions earlier and had more fun in the process.

David Meerman Scott
Wall Street Journal *best-selling author of thirteen books, including* The New Rules of Marketing and PR

Steve and Erin are two deep thinkers and sincere practitioners whose decades of work on themselves and with their clients has given them a profound vantage point from which to help others. This book is an abundant harvest of their combined learning about how to break stagnation and catalyze immense growth in any area of your life.

Craig Hamilton
Founder, The Practice of Direct Awakening

This book is a must-read for anyone who wants to set and achieve audacious goals, overcome failure, and live a visionary life. The authors guide you through a personalized and practical approach to goal-setting, including the 5R framework, a powerful tool to plan, execute, and even rest your way to success. The book is full of engaging stories and insights that will challenge and inspire you to live your unique vision in the world.

Eldon Sprickerhoff
Strategic advisor, Caledon Ventures

Few individuals know and love the territory of transformation like Erin and Steve. The fruit of their hard-won experience shines through in *Superabound* as they walk the reader through smart, original, and easy-to-understand tools for turning big dreams into bigger realities. An encouraging tonic for those seeking friendly and inspiring counsel on their life journey.

Carter Phipps

Author of Evolutionaries *and coauthor of*
Conscious Leadership

SUPERABOUND

LIVE THE LIFE THE UNIVERSE
IS DREAMING FOR YOU

SUPERABOUND

ERIN AQUIN + STEVE HAASE

Advantage | Books

Published by Advantage Books, Charleston, South Carolina.
An imprint of Advantage Media.

ADVANTAGE is a registered trademark, and the Advantage colophon is a trademark of Advantage Media Group, Inc.

Printed in the United States of America.

10 9 8 7 6 5 4 3 2 1

ISBN: 979-8-89188-021-4 (Hardcover)
ISBN: 979-8-89188-022-1 (eBook)

Library of Congress Control Number: 2024902814

Cover design by Matthew Morse.
Layout design by Ruthie Wood.
Photography by Jessi McConnell @jessthesnapper.

This publication is designed to provide accurate and authoritative information in regard to the subject matter covered. It is sold with the understanding that the publisher is not engaged in rendering legal, accounting, or other professional services. If legal advice or other expert assistance is required, the services of a competent professional person should be sought.

Advantage Books is an imprint of Advantage Media Group. Advantage Media helps busy entrepreneurs, CEOs, and leaders write and publish a book to grow their business and become the authority in their field. Advantage authors comprise an exclusive community of industry professionals, idea-makers, and thought leaders. For more information go to **advantagemedia.com**.

For Audrey and Julian, may you bravely climb your mountains.

CONTENTS

FOREWORD

My father was a traditional corporate man, earning a Harvard Business School MBA, which led to senior positions in multinational companies. Growing up in the leafy New York City suburbs, all my parents' friends were on the same path and we kids were expected to do the same. Good schools, a big job, country clubs, and a nice house.

I started down that well-worn route to perceived success too, working on Wall Street after graduating from university with an economics degree. When I started my career, I fully expected to work a few years and then get my own MBA just like my father had done.

The problem was that I hated finance. I realized that I had to find something more interesting. Unlike most people, I was open to the signals coming from somewhere deep in my mind. When faced with forks in the career road, I started choosing the direction that appeared to be the most fun, not the one that was the most prestigious name on a business card or the one that made the most money.

At age twenty-six I found myself all alone in Tokyo opening the Asia-Pacific office of an economic consultancy. My father and my friends told me I was nuts, that the international offices of US companies were backwaters. However, I was enjoying life far away from company headquarters and ended up building a remarkable life in Asia over nearly a decade, starting a family, enjoying myself, and living the perfect life for me.

Upon moving back to my own country, I once again did what was expected because I was fearful of having enough money to raise my young family. I took a corporate job at a technology company, rising through the ranks to become vice president of marketing. I hated having bosses, well, bossing me. But I sucked it up and did OK. However, I wasn't happy at work because I wasn't having much fun. A few years later, the company was acquired by a much larger organization, and I was fired. Sacked. My marketing ideas were a little too radical for my new bosses.

While I didn't use the term "universe" at the time, the way that Steve and Erin do in this book, I knew that there was something missing in my career. Something in my mind was telling me I had more to offer. The world was a big, fun, interesting place, and I was being held back by trying to fit into the status quo.

So, I started writing books, speaking at events, and advising emerging companies on how to align marketing with the ways that people buy. That was back in 2002, and since then, my thirteen books have sold over a million copies in thirty languages. I'm invited to speak all over the world and (so far) have delivered talks in more than forty countries and on all seven continents.

I'm living the life that the universe is dreaming for me! I haven't had a boss in more than two decades and I can pick and choose the projects that are the most fun.

In this excellent book, Erin and Steve will show you how to do the same. They share how you can achieve remarkable things and make your dreams a reality. I wish I had the ideas in *Superabound* when I was struggling early in my own career because I would have found my passions earlier and would have had more fun in the process.

The universe has big dreams for you too, so turn the page to begin your own journey to a more fulfilling life.

—David Meerman Scott, business growth strategist and *Wall Street Journal* best-selling author of thirteen books, including *The New Rules of Marketing and PR*

CHAPTER 1

The Invitation

Erin's Breakdown

Part of me felt relieved as I looked at the ultrasound images before me. While the doctor explained what she saw, I finally had proof that my suffering was not just a hallucination.

For the past six months I'd dealt with a mysterious pain and joint swelling. It started in one knee and, over the course of a few weeks, spread throughout my entire body, making it painful to walk and hard to lift anything heavier than a teacup. After several trips to urgent care, tearful meetings with my family doctor, round after round of inconclusive bloodwork, and one visit to a specialist that insisted I would end up in a wheelchair before my thirty-first birthday, another expert and researcher agreed to see me and provide a second opinion.

Seeing the evidence from within my body that there was something creating all this pain and immobility was strangely comforting, that is until we began to discuss the common medications used to treat this condition. I wasn't against medical intervention, but the drugs used to treat conditions like mine were essentially low doses of chemotherapy. This gave me pause.

When the doctor explained I would need to have my liver and kidneys tested regularly, and that if I was planning on having children I would need to be off the medication for at least a year before getting pregnant, I knew this was a serious decision. Because the doctor knew my background as a yoga teacher and acupuncturist, she suggested I use my holistic tool kit first and then come to a decision I could feel peace around.

I went home that day feeling the opposite of peace and reached out to my friend, Jeff Carreira. Jeff is an internationally renowned meditation teacher and someone I trust. He has the rare gift of being able to speak the hard truth and have it feel like love. As we spoke, I broke down.

"I finally have my yoga business and acupuncture practice built up and now I can hardly make it up the stairs, let alone teach," I sobbed. "Plus what am I going to do about my engagement to Steve? It's not fair to him to get married now knowing how sick I am and what that might mean for our future."

Without dismissing my fear or trying to brush my pain aside, Jeff offered me a different perspective. First, he agreed that it had been a lot of work to build what I had in my business and personal life. But then he asked a question I hadn't considered: "What if the worst thing you can imagine right now—being sick and in a wheelchair before the end of the year—is actually an opportunity to do something that never would have been available without this health issue?"

Had anyone else posed this question at that particular moment I would have hung up the phone. For months, people had been offering me tidy clichés that totally diminished my suffering. "Everything happens for a reason" or "Maybe this is all part of some bigger mystical plan" were not doing it for me, regardless of how well-meaning the people sharing this advice tried to be.

Jeff's question was different, and not because of the words but because of what I felt within them. I knew Jeff as someone who thought deeply about life and experienced awe in the face of the vastness of the Universe. That made me start to wonder how I felt. If I believed the Universe was a good place to be and that perhaps it was even on my side, how might this current limitation be something other than the worst thing that ever happened to me? And how could it be the beginning of something I didn't know was possible?

This moment of mental gymnastics opened my perspective and was an organic introduction to the power of mindset work. The possibility that every obstacle may be a nudge toward a new and more important path I hadn't yet discovered made me less frustrated by my situation and more attentive to the possibilities that surrounded me.

Steve's Moment of Truth

When Erin first started having health problems, we were in a long-distance relationship in two different countries. It was hard, since we spent our time apart planning the next time we'd be together and our time together was overshadowed by a sad countdown to when we would be apart again.

We knew we had a good thing going and would someday be together, in the same place, building the magical life we knew was possible. The questions were simply when and where.

So, it shocked me when she said over the phone one day, not long after we got engaged, "You don't have to go through with this."

"With what?" I asked.

"Getting married, having me in your life. The whole thing. You shouldn't be held back by someone who is broken."

I was silent. It felt like her constant pain and physical limitations had started to give way to signs of depression as well. I still wanted Erin in my life. But she was changing. What if she was right and our dreams of a future filled with joy and adventure were never to be? Was I signing up to be her caretaker before we'd even lived a full week together? Suddenly I wasn't so sure about it all.

It felt scary committing to a path that could contain much more pain than I had originally expected. Pushing my thirty-year-old wife around in a wheelchair was not something I had put in my life plan at that point.

And major choices around having kids and career path were suddenly forced upon us before we were ready.

I took a slow, shaky breath and connected with the deepest knowing I could access at the time. A voice within me said, "You don't know exactly what lies ahead. But Erin's essence is still in there and the spiritual connection you share is stronger than this challenging moment."

I couldn't rely on Erin's health to improve, and yet I had a sense that we had meaningful path ahead.

So I made a decision, one that I knew would have big implications for our future.

I took another breath and said, "I'm not going anywhere. It's *you* I love, and I want to be with you however you are."

"Are you sure?" she said.

"Yes. You can scratch your worries about me off your list and use your energy to focus on your health instead."

That wasn't the last time the question of whether we should stay together came up, either from Erin or replayed within my own mind.

But after that point I fundamentally knew where I stood. I was staying. I wanted to do this. That knowledge gave me clarity even amid the fear, sadness, or anxiety that would emerge as thoughts of our uncertain future entered my mind.

Looking back on it, I still can't pinpoint why I was able to trust that things would turn out, to the point that I was even willing to upend my life for it. I couldn't see the top of the mountain that we were on, but I had enough confidence in the vision of our relationship and, to be honest, the stubbornness to take on the challenges at hand, that we were able to keep going.

Why This Matters

You might be wondering, "*Why start a book about achieving goals with an overly personal, kind of spiritual tale about a health scare in a long-distance relationship?*" There are a few reasons.

First, we want to introduce ourselves to you as real people. Just like you, Erin and I have had tough moments and important crossroads to navigate. We don't pretend to have life wrapped up in a pretty bow, which means we have a lot of practice using the very tools we are going to share.

The next reason is because there's power in seeing difficult situations—like a health issue or the separation of a long-distance relationship—as opportunities for growth. Tough moments give you a chance to test your resolve and become stronger. It would have been easy to throw in the towel on our relationship because of a diagnosis, but we would have missed the growth that comes from orienting our lives toward an important vision.

As such, this is not a typical business or personal development book. We're not going to overwhelm you with case studies or not-so-subtle sales pitches trying to convince you to hire us or speak at your next conference. Don't get me wrong, Erin and I love presenting and working with clients. But the purpose of this book is to help leaders and entrepreneurs make their dreams a reality, regardless of what challenges may lie ahead.

Throughout this book you will find we've woven a metaphorical story about hiking up a mountain at night, because that is what bringing your plans to life in the world sometimes feels like. While anyone can benefit from what we share, it is business owners and leaders we feel most compelled to support because they are doing the impossible, sometimes being the only people in the world who believe in the importance of their vision.

It is also important that you know, we didn't create these tools out of thin air for the purpose of this book. The Superabound method has taken shape over years and has helped us go from freelance yoga teacher and corporate worker bee to two of the most well-respected coaches in our community and cofounders of a thriving business where we have weekends off and epic vacations with our two young kids. These tools have helped us be a better team in so many ways. As business cofounders who are married with two children, you can bet what you're about to learn has been road tested under some extreme conditions, both personal and professional.

Most importantly, the Superabound method has successfully helped our clients do what had once been unimaginable to them, including:

- Quitting the corporate job, moving to a beach, and working remotely (you know, the Instagram dream)

- Growing a promising part-time business into a million-dollar company

- Creating a culture of teamwork so strong that the CEO finally took a month-long vacation

Reading and implementing the tools in this book will support you as a whole person, not just as the leader of a company or in the various roles you juggle.

If that sounds like the kind of abundance you want in your life, let's get ready for an adventure.

Preparing to Hike the Mountain

"Why would you ever hike up that mountain at night?"

The skeptic's words needle you as you pack your gear. It does seem a bit extreme. The mountain is dark, it gets cold at elevation, and you've never been up there before. But something deep inside you is drawn to it, almost as if the mountain itself is calling you forward.

You feel a sense of destiny when you think about that cold, remote place—which seems strange because everyone is telling you how nice it is right here where you live. But what they call a normal life doesn't feel right to you. So, you zip your bag and head out the door, knowing it won't be easy but it might be magical.

CHAPTER 2

What Is Superabounding?

By Steve

To Superabound is to align your life with your dreams. It means doing the work, both inner and outer, to stop pushing the things that matter most off into a distant future and start making progress on them now.

Many people don't choose where they put their energy and attention. They live their life according to cultural norms and expectations, rarely venturing outside their given roles. They may sense a pull to something different, but they stay put. After all, it's easier to be in the status quo than to step back and question the life you've built in order to fit in.

But fitting in comes at a cost.

Rather than feeling free to explore your unique interests and talents, maybe you train and work in a field that your family would approve of. Rather than living a lifestyle you prefer, you opt to repeat whatever is most common in your dominant culture. Maybe you present yourself in a way that is palatable to others in your profession rather than sharing what you really think and feel.

> **To Superabound is to align your life with your dreams.**

The worst part is that while you spend your life fitting into the way other people expect you to be, you never make a unique contribution to the world. This book is for people who don't want to pay that price anymore but may not be sure how to break out of the stronghold of the status quo.

What It Takes

The first step to Superabounding is to get more flexible about what you think you know. For instance, what would happen if you started looking for patterns and purpose in the Universe? In Erin's situation it meant exploring the possibilities of her challenges being a door to new opportunities.

Increasing the flexibility of your thinking can connect you to a deeper purpose for your life as you consider, even if just for a moment, that you were meant for great things. Or, as Erin and I like to say, that there is a life the Universe is dreaming for you.

Now, about the word "Superabound." It is not one we made up. If you look up the word Superabound in a dictionary, you'll find some variation of "overflowing with abundance."

The most important part about that abundance is not the way it looks to other people, but the way it feels to you. I'm always fascinated by stories of the ultra-wealthy who are consumed with jealousy over one of their friends or peers having even more than they do. They may have money, but they don't have the inner wealth of purpose, connection, and well-being that you will discover in this book.

Financial success can be fun, and these tools can help you achieve it, if that's your desire. But more important is to create a life you find fulfilling on all levels: physical, relational, emotional, mental, and spiritual.

Superabounding is like hiking up a mountain in the middle of the night. You may not know exactly where you're going, and you can't see all the terrain you need to cross. But something is calling you toward that shrouded peak, and there are lanterns on the path for you to light that will illuminate what's next for you.

In other words, trust is a key ingredient in Superabounding. Trust in yourself, that you can accomplish remarkable things. Trust in the process, that taking consistently aligned steps will move you toward your next milestone. And trust in the Universe, that there's more going on here than you could ever know or understand. When you pay attention to the signs around you and within you, magical things can happen.

Finally, trust that you are worthy of Superabundance. You are not just your name, your history, your skills, or your appearance. You are a singular instance of cosmic creativity, inseparable from the source itself. As such, you are worthy of everything that this mysterious creativity has to offer.

Applying the principles in this book to your life will not only make your own path richer but will inspire others with what's possible as well. That's what happened with Erin's healing and recovery. Her realization that she needed to find a new way of working and living became the catalyst for starting a coaching business that we now work in together. Not only has that business made $1,000,000 in under three years, the tools and techniques we developed along the way have helped countless entrepreneurs to create financial autonomy in their own businesses without overworking and burning out.

But rather than give you a prescriptive plan, this book will be your guide as you learn to navigate your own path, illuminate it along the way, and deal with the struggles—both inner and outer—that you will no doubt face.

What Do We Mean by "The Universe"?

By Erin

We use the word "Universe" throughout the book, and you might be wondering what we mean when we say that. So, a short definition is in order.

Steve and I are both longtime spiritual practitioners. We met in a meditation community and have spent plenty of time in our relationship studying the mystical. When creating our company, we knew we wanted it to be a warm and inclusive place, especially for leaders and business owners who were tired of compartmentalizing their lives in ways where they couldn't bring their full spiritual selves to the table.

To that end, we use the word "Universe" as a nod to the mystical, scientific, and divine while remaining intentionally open for you to interpret it in the way that makes most sense to you. While we hope to offer you a new way of approaching and achieving your goals, this isn't a book with an ulterior motive to get our spiritual beliefs to become yours. So, we will use the word "Universe" and invite you to let that mean whatever is most aligned and supportive to you.

How to Get the Most from This Book

There are a few limitations to teaching you the Superabound method in a book. Unlike a coaching session or a workshop, we can't help you draw out your worthy vision and align your daily life and business to it.

Therefore you, the reader, are going to have to be your own champion for this part, using this book as your guiding tool. You must be the one to decide to engage with the exercises and treat this text like a powerful training program to help you build the strength and inner resources to get you all the way to your next big milestone.

We have done our best to keep it interesting and you will notice that the sections start with who is writing it. We chose to author our sections individually so you could get the full benefit of each of our voices and experiences, rather than needing to squish our quirks into a lifeless "we" throughout the book.

You will get even more out of the book and the exercises if you share your learning and reach out for support through the free resources we have waiting for you at *www.beSuperabound.com/collective*.

There's a community of entrepreneurs, leaders, and visionaries who are also using these principles to Superabound in their own lives. The journey is better with friends, and you'll find some in this collective. We hope you'll be inspired to join us there.

Avoid the Goal Swamp

"The mountain is dangerous," your taxi driver says as he honks and swerves between scooters, heavy trucks, and wooden carts on the road to where you'll be starting your climb.

"Many people don't even go up the mountain after they see it. I don't know why. There's a vast swamp at the bottom that is no less dangerous than the climb.

"The mountain is tricky. The ground can suddenly give way beneath you, or you'll find yourself right between a momma bear and her cub, and most people don't notice until it's too late.

"Even still," he shrugs, "most people walk around in circles at the bottom and stay there."

Your stomach does a flip, and you continue the rest of the ride in silence, until finally you pull into the park entrance. You climb out of the car, your legs unsure beneath you. The driver calls out, "Good luck, and don't get stuck walking around the bottom," before driving away.

CHAPTER 3

The Hidden Risks
of Goals

By Erin

I walked into the bar rehearsing the excuse I would use for leaving early. It was only Wednesday but I had already been to a few other shows earlier in the week and this was one I wasn't looking forward to. The bar was busy, not a bad sign, and I recognized a few talent agents and managers I knew from the local music scene. But I wrote off their presence. It was part of their job to go to band showcases like this one. They did it all the time hoping they would find a hidden gem in the form of an up-and-coming group they could add to their roster.

My reason for being there was not because it was part of my job, but out of obligation. I promised a new friend and his bandmates at an industry party that I would come to see their next show. At the time I agreed, I had enjoyed a few gin and tonics and, even in my buzzed state, I immediately regretted it.

But a promise is a promise and after a couple years of working for radio stations, promoters, and bands, I knew what kind of challenge this group was facing on their path to success. I figured the least I could do was show up and be another body in the room to support them.

The lights went down, and I said my usual silent prayer to the Gods-of-Bands-Never-Seen-Live:

"May these songs be passable,
May your singer have perfect pitch,
May your bassist never have duck lips
And if it is not to be, let this set be short!"

I held my breath for the first verse. So far, so good. The song was really fun. My new friend Adrian was a fantastic and charismatic singer, and the bass player was a gorgeous woman who made zero weird faces. By the time the set was over, I knew this group had something special.

The more I got to know Adrian and his band the more impressed I was. They were all incredibly driven and clear on their goal to get signed by a record company and make a chart-topping album.

They were so clear, in fact, that the band lived together in order to reduce distractions. They rehearsed daily and financially supported Adrian so he didn't have to work and could focus entirely on the band. His job was to write amazing songs and make the connections needed to secure a record deal while the rest of them worked in bars and took other odd jobs between shows.

By now you might be wondering what uber-famous band I am giving you the backstory of, but sadly this is not one of those tales. Despite the talent, drive, and seemingly clear goal Adrian and his band had, they were still humans like the rest of us.

Adrian soon found himself struggling under the pressure of trying to write new material week after week. To make things more stressful he felt he had to justify every penny he spent to each member of the band since they were paying his share of the bills. His bandmates became resentful that he wasn't writing better songs or landing them a record deal while they exhausted themselves trying to juggle their many jobs to cover his part of the expenses.

Over time, the tension became too much, and they started fighting at home and in rehearsal. The whole arrangement turned rotten, and they eventually broke up.

Stuck in the Swamp

It's easy to read this story and think, "Well, that makes sense. Most bands never make it big." But while it's true the music industry can be tough, competitive, and hard to predict, this band didn't fall apart simply because the industry is unkind. This group was barely at the starting line of the journey they would need to endure in order to see their goal realized.

They fell apart not from any external cause but from approaching their goal in the standard, and rather unhelpful, way. They were stuck in what Steve and I call the "Goal Swamp."

The Goal Swamp is where great business ideas go to die, where people lose momentum and go around in circles on their good intentions for their health and fitness. Being in the Goal Swamp feels hard and you lose energy without going anywhere because you must fight to lift your legs for every single step.

No doubt you've experienced this in your own life. You set your sights on something for reasons you don't fully understand, underestimate how challenging the journey will get, then show up for the challenge without the tools you need to make real progress.

If you think all it takes to reach a goal is to simply choose a thing you want to do, line up all the steps, show up for each of those things, and expect all your wildest dreams to come true, you are missing something very important. Like Adrian and his band, you might get derailed before you even get started.

No matter how neat and tidy your goals are, life rarely unfolds the way you plan it. Because of this, it's your reaction to the twists and turns along the way that becomes the deciding factor on whether you continue to pursue your goals or give up, sacrificing your self-worth and your boots to the Goal Swamp.

Let's say you haven't worked out for many years and then wake up one morning and decide that your new goal is to bench press 100 pounds more than you did at the peak of your athletic power. Just for fun, let's also imagine you had the body of a human and the mind of a robot.

No matter how neat and tidy your goals are, life rarely unfolds the way you plan it.

In that case, you would calculate the window of time it might take to reach this goal, then program three to five days of weight training and supplemental routines to keep your body mobile and injury free. You would change your diet to eat only nutrient-rich foods to support your goal and you would sleep eight to nine hours a night. You would also book a full physical to make sure there were no pesky human issues that could get in the way of your epic life. Once you got the green light from your doctor you would also hire a top-tier trainer and physical therapist to help you prevent injuries that could slow down your progress. Within the reasonable time frame you had calculated, your goal would be achieved.

Most goal setting looks similar to this. It's made for people who have suddenly been given the mind of a robot. In reality, the same goal with the body *and* mind of a human (which you and every reader of this book has, by the way) would probably look more like this. First, you guess how long it should take to reach your bench press goal based on something you overheard at a party. Then you go online to see what a popular fitness influencer says is the best way to train and you start their YouTube regimen.

You add some protein powder to your diet but don't make any significant changes to what you eat because you are just trying to bench press more, not become a walking health food store. You miss about half of your planned workouts because going to the gym in the morning sucks and you are sore. You skip meeting with your doctor because you don't need medical clearance. It's not the Olympics after all. And forget the trainer, PT, or massage therapist because really, who has that kind of time?

If this sounds at all familiar to you, you know what happens next. Over the coming weeks you go to the gym less and less, swear off protein powder for life, and end up in the care of a physiotherapist to deal with all the injuries you acquired during your on-again off-again YouTube bootcamp.

The problem for most people is not the goal itself, but in the space between what you plan in moments of inspiration, and the reality of your human life where energy, determination, and self-belief fluctuate daily. To make it worse, you might have been taught that your self-worth is tethered to your achievements and accomplishments. So, when you set a goal and don't find a way to reach it, it can be a devastating blow to your confidence.

Knowing the Dangers

I am not against having big dreams. In fact I've spent much of my adult life helping people make their wildest dreams a reality. What I am against is the way we've been taught to approach them. Regardless of whether you are trying to create a chart-topping album or work out like a gladiator, one thing is clear: the old way of setting goals almost never works and can leave you worse off than when you started.

That's why, before you can reframe your goals into what we call Lanterns and then work toward them, you must understand the dangers of being in the Goal Swamp so you can stay out of it.

Have you ever gotten to the end of a major project or reached something you thought was a big goal and felt completely empty inside? It's when you finally get the degree you've been working toward only to discover you have no desire to be in that field. Or when you race toward the next mile marker and realize you've been so deep in your own world that you've lost connection with the people who actually make the journey worthwhile.

The Goal Swamp is when you're making enormous amounts of effort, step after step, but only seeing inches of real progress. The progress is slow and painful, and it only takes you deeper into the swamp. When you're in the Goal Swamp, the view never changes. You just get colder and more tired.

When it comes to goals, most people are wasting their life's energy trudging through the Goal Swamp instead of going up a mountain they intend to climb. It's hard to overflow with abundance, to Super-abound, when your boots are stuck in the mud.

You need to be able to spot when you're in the swamp, and there are four dangers to look out for. Understanding them and being honest with yourself about the ones that are most likely to trip you up will make everything that follows in this process much easier.

The four dangers are:

1. Status Seeking

2. Racing the Clock

3. The Blinders of Doom

4. Confusing a Goal for your Vision

Danger #1: Status Seeking

Humans are social creatures. From an early age you were probably taught that when you do things others approve of, you receive praise and when you don't you get scolded. Steve and I have two children who are six and eight at the time of this writing.

Our eight-year-old has already figured out that she increases her chances of getting what she wants when she is helpful around the house. If I go into her room in the morning and the bed is made, she is dressed and ready for school, with her reading done and toys tidy in the basement, I can almost guarantee she is about to ask me for something she wants.

Our six-year-old, on the other hand, has not yet mastered this social tactic and can tear apart a room while he simultaneously asks

Transactional approval from a young age breeds status-seeking behavior later in life.

to watch his favorite show or eat ice cream for dinner. He hasn't figured out what our older child knows: that it is harder for us to say no to a request when she has accomplished or exceeded the basic things we expect her to do around the house as part of family teamwork.

As a life coach, I cringe a bit knowing my kids are learning these social games. On the one hand, I absolutely want my children to contribute and not expect that they can have special things delivered on a regular basis without doing some age-appropriate tasks. On the other, I know that many children grow up to confuse the praise they get for their accomplishments with love and purpose. And transactional approval from a young age breeds status-seeking behavior later in life.

Consider this for yourself. Are you someone who has learned to perform or achieve based on what you think others will approve of, or are you working on things that are personally meaningful?

You might find there's friction between the two. Being respected and admired feels good, especially by people who matter deeply to you. And a clear path to impressing those people is to collect the accolades that matter to them. However, pursuing goals only for the sake of increasing your status will leave you feeling empty in moments you expected to feel fulfilled.

Steve and I have worked with some of the world's most talented musicians, medical experts, and entrepreneurs whose products and services have made life better for countless people. There is a distinct difference in confidence, personal trust, and self-worth between people who are working on goals that are in alignment with their own vision and those who are following a path their parents, teachers, or mentors prescribed.

The good news is that this book will help you identify your true Vision, the one that has little to do with anyone else's expectations. And if you are like most of the people we have led through this process you will quickly find yourself dropping goals you set merely to increase your status. Instead, your focus will turn to those that light the way toward the big vision you have for your life.

Adrian and his band had the goal of making a hit album so they could become superstars. They loved music, but getting on stage show after show with the intention to be seen by the "right" record company executive drained them. Grasping for that specific outcome when they could have simply enjoyed making music together surely shortened their life span as a band. It does the same for almost anyone who chooses a goal in order to increase their status.

YOUR TURN

- If no one—not even your parents or partner—would ever know that you reached your goal, would you still pursue it?

- Would your future self, looking back on a long life, be proud of you for achieving this goal or would they feel a sense of regret for what it cost to get there?

Danger #2: Racing the Clock

Goals and deadlines. We are so used to seeing these two tempestuous frenemies together that many people pin dates on every goal, big and small. And while there are those who claim due dates are a strong motivator, I would argue there are far better sources of inspiration out there.

If you happen to be one of the rare people who loves how deadlines look and feel, then I'm happy for you. Don't change a thing. If, however, you feel that adding an arbitrary date to an already challenging goal is stressful, this one is for you.

Shannin Williams is the founder and CEO of The Bertrand Williams School of Design Visualization. She is not only a sought-after architectural illustrator and interior designer, but when I first began coaching Shannin, she was feeling stuck, working in an organization that had become dysfunctional.

"I have always been someone who marched to the beat of my own drum," Shannin told me. So instead of wasting more years behind a desk working in a place she didn't feel appreciated, she started an online business teaching the lost art of hand drawing skills to other designers. Her initial launches went well, and so she set a revenue target as a way of proving the ongoing viability of her business and to create a healthy financial cushion to leave her nine-to-five job with.

We spent time on one session talking about whether she should choose a date to go along with her goal. At the time, Shannin was in a group with new entrepreneurs and saw many of her peers pinning deadlines on their monetary goals, insisting that it was important to do so. But Shannin had a gut feeling that a deadline would distract her. Instead, she wanted to focus on refining her programs and converting qualified leads into paying clients. During that session, she decided not to try to use time as her motivator, but instead tap into her passion and vision and work from there.

> **Tacking an arbitrary deadline onto a brand-new venture is like doing business on "hard mode."**

While her peers frantically pushed for every dollar instead of making good business decisions for the long term, Shannin worked on delighting her students and creating smoother processes for her business. She watched her friends shaming themselves over missing their made-up timelines and taking no joy in what they had achieved. This is the problem with racing the clock and a telltale sign you're in the Goal Swamp.

Tacking an arbitrary deadline onto a brand-new venture is like doing business on "hard mode."

In many cases, the problem isn't the goal itself. It's using time as a motivator and placing huge expectations on a project at the worst possible point: the beginning.

Shannin's peers were doing what many do when they set goals. Even though they were at a point in their journey where they knew virtually nothing about what it would take to start their own business and make hundreds of thousands of dollars, they decided to amplify the difficulty by trying to beat the clock while doing it.

Knowing she had never created a financial buffer to leave her job, Shannin didn't add the pressure of a looming deadline. Instead of making her challenge even harder, she focused instead on creating a business that could easily reach her magic number. The inspiration to achieve her goal was the dream of going full time in her own business. That was far more inspiring to her than a random day in April she made up as the date she must do it by.

Equally as important, this allowed Shannin to stay focused on making responsive decisions that moved her business forward and better served her clients. Where racing the clock leads many business owners to make reactive, short-term decisions, Shannin was able to be thoughtful and strategic.

Interestingly, although she wasn't focused on reaching her revenue goal by a specific date, she did it so swiftly that she was financially equipped to quit her nine-to-five job months before she expected to do so. Now, full time in her business, with students and clients around the world, Shannin continues to grow her revenue year after year without harsh deadlines. She chooses goals that will support her, her clients, and her business for the long term—no added time pressure required.

Take a moment to answer the following for yourself:

- Do you have a goal with a deadline attached to it?

- If so, how does that deadline feel as you get deeper into the project or learn more about your goal?

- Are you trying to beat the clock in a way that feels inspiring or feels like a risky bet?

- Would you choose that same deadline for yourself if you were to set it right now?

Again, if you feel right on track and that trying to beat the clock is supporting you, congratulations. If not, it might be because you made plans when you didn't yet know what you didn't know. This is rarely a good strategy and might lead to a sense of impending doom as the date gets closer.

Danger #3: The Blinders of Doom

The Blinders of Doom is an especially dangerous pitfall because it can hurt you both in the Goal Swamp and while you are hiking up the mountain toward your vision. Essentially the blinders are a "do whatever it takes" attitude that blocks your peripheral view to focus solely on the path in front of you.

While focus isn't a bad thing, the Blinders of Doom offer such a reduced perspective that it's like looking through a peephole while navigating precarious terrain. Not only do you miss the scenery along the way, but you won't notice the crocodile stalking you (if you are in the Goal Swamp) or the sharp drop off the cliff (if you managed to make it to the mountain).

It might seem dramatic to call them Blinders of Doom, but the effect of wearing them is serious and devastating for those who do. In our time as coaches, we have heard countless stories from people who came face-to-face with the consequences. Some of those real-life cases include:

- A start-up founder whose business was finally taking off only to be told that their partner was sick of waiting for them to come home night after night and wanted a divorce.

- The mother who had been working evenings and weekends to reach her financial milestone. When she excitedly shared the news with her family that she did it, instead of celebrating, her child responded, "You love your business more than us don't you, Mommy?"

- Or in my case, working hard to have my first truly successful year only to burn out and go through a chronic illness that subsequently shut down the business I had spent a decade building.

YOUR TURN

These situations are tough, and while there is always more to the story, it is important to be honest with yourself about your approach to your goals. Even if you don't think of yourself as someone who puts blinders on when it comes to your next milestone, the following questions will help you maintain perspective:

- When you are focused on a goal, what important things sometimes take a back seat? For many people it is some form of self-care that gets axed from their calendar (exercise, sleep, eating well). What is it for you?

- What feedback do you get most often from the people you love and respect in your life when you are working toward a major goal?

- Whom can you trust to tell you the truth when you have the Blinders of Doom on?

An early warning sign that you may have blinders on is that the people in your life start complaining about it. For me, a telltale sign I am wearing the Blinders of Doom comes from my kids.

Although I don't do this often, like many business owners I will occasionally go down a rabbit hole working on something outside my regular hours. When my kids notice me making the repeated claim that I "just need ten more minutes," they call my bluff. They set an alarm and deliver a solid guilt trip if I don't close my computer the moment the buzzer goes off.

> **An early warning sign that you may have blinders on is that the people in your life start complaining about it.**

If Blinders of Doom are something that is real for you, the way to avoid that danger is to find ways to gradually expand your perspective. Here are a few things that help us keep the blinders off.

First, Steve and I set aside time each week where it's just the two of us and we're not allowed to talk about work or business. You may find that locking your computer away for a set period or having a tech-free day each week helps you remove the blinders. Sometimes all you need is a deliberate step back to prevent catastrophe from taking root in your life. This doesn't have to be fancy. I prefer a thirty-minute walk with my headphones on and some great tunes. This time reminds me that my life is much bigger than any milestone in front of me.

Another source of support for people working on big goals is community. Doing something epic is often lonely. If one of the things you're doing is running a business, we invite you to join the Superabound Collective to connect with other business owners. Head over to *beSuperabound.com/collective* to learn more.

Danger #4: Confusing Goals with Your Vision

This final danger when trying to achieve a goal is one that can be harder to spot but is no less important to understand than the others, especially in the moments you fail to achieve what you wanted. Ideally as you learn to pursue only those goals that are aligned with your purpose in life, your milestones will move you further along the path toward real fulfillment and impact.

But the truth is you're probably going to fail plenty of times. And the moment you mistake a small failure, such as not achieving a goal, with the mega failure of not achieving your overall Vision, you may feel like all is lost and give up, instead of looking for another path up the mountain.

For instance, Steve and I have a shared vision in our business and our life: *to help people realize the life the Universe is dreaming for them.* This is not a goal. There is no box to check at the end of the year that says we have completed it and can move on to the next project.

This is a very high-level, top-of-the-mountain vision (which we will help you find for yourself in the next part of this book). To move closer to that vision, we have goals, or what we think of as unlit lanterns, on the path ahead and we are constantly working toward them. One specific lantern we have taken steps to light over the past year is publishing the book you are reading right now.

Steve and I are committed to supporting as many people as possible who want to learn the Superabound tools and one of those ways is putting our work into a book that can be read by people all over the world. But that took a very intentional, vision-driven journey.

In fact, before we decided that coauthoring this book was a lantern we wanted to light, Steve and I were both working on separate book projects—his more focused on management strategies for start-ups while mine was for entrepreneurs who wanted to bring more magic and spiritual energy to their business. I was about 80 percent through my first draft when Steve asked the question: "Does it make sense for us to be working on these two separate books? I know they will help people get a couple useful tools, but is this the best way we can help more people live the life the Universe is dreaming for them?"

It took no more than a five-minute conversation for us both to agree we needed to set aside the projects we had each poured hundreds of hours into and start again. Getting this book out of our heads and into the hands of readers all around the world is one lantern lit. And yet, even though I am proud of us for getting here, lighting this lantern is not the purpose of my life or business. I didn't just pack my bags on release day and say "Well, that's all the contribution I need to make. Good luck from here, world. Enjoy the book!"

This book is just one more lantern we have lit on the mountain we are climbing. The same is true for you. Your next goal, or lantern, is not the purpose of your life. It doesn't make you a more worthy person when you reach it, or an inadequate one if you take another path.

If, however, you confuse a specific milestone with achieving your life's purpose, you put yourself in a difficult position. You're either going to achieve it and feel underwhelmed to realize you are only halfway up a mountain you might not even want to be on. Or if you don't reach that milestone you will feel like a complete failure and that you've been wasting your life.

YOUR TURN

Think about a goal you're working toward.

Now imagine you spend the next two years on it and you're not able to meet it. What would you make that mean about you and your effort?

If you discovered that particular goal was no longer an option in this lifetime for you, how easy would it be for you to create a fulfilling life?

A big clue that you're confusing one goal with the entire point for your life is a lack of creativity. If it would be hard to picture pivoting beyond an unrealized dream, then you may actually be in the Goal Swamp.

My friend Adrian confused the goal of getting a record deal with his life's purpose. When a manager or A&R rep would come to a show, he was filled with hope. But when that person didn't offer to meet with the band to discuss their next steps he would deflate. This emotional roller coaster chipped away at Adrian's confidence and sapped his energy when it came to songwriting or courting the various industry gatekeepers.

Even if he had been able to lock down his dream recording contract before the band imploded, plenty of bands at that time had contracts that were never activated or whose records were made but sat on a shelf collecting dust and were never released. Adrian had a clear goal in wanting the contract, but since he elevated it to the status of his purpose for performing and creating music, he cut himself off from other creative ways to move his career forward—the ones that didn't involve signing with a label and making a record the traditional way.

It's so important to understand the four dangers of goal setting *before* you set off on your night hike. Unless you're on the lookout for the ways in which you may be status seeking, putting arbitrary and unhelpful dates on your milestones, wearing Blinders of Doom, or mistaking your goals for your vision, the tools in this book won't help you Superabound.

It's time to climb out of the Goal Swamp and discover a better way to think about goals.

Lanterns Await

The sky grows darker and with each passing moment more and more stars begin to gently flicker. You can make out the shape of the mountain before you because unlike the bejeweled sky, the mountain appears in the landscape like a blank void in which no stars shine.

But you know that along the path there are beacons standing strong in the cold dark, waiting to receive and amplify the flame of the torch you'll be carrying as your only source of light.

These as-yet unlit lanterns will become your milestones, shining proof that you are making progress up the mountain.

And if you're willing to keep moving forward and light them, the lanterns will also illuminate the way for those who will come after you.

CHAPTER 4

Trading Your Goals for Lanterns

By Steve

From here on we're going to be evolving our approach to goals by using the word "Lanterns" and illuminating all that the word entails. Lanterns are the mile markers on the path to living a life you are proud of, and they open up a new way to think about important achievements.

By now you know that we're not big fans of the way most people choose and use goals. And because the word "goal" carries so much baggage, rather than trying to massage it into something more helpful, we're going to throw it out entirely.

It may seem like semantics, but words have power. And we've seen how impactful this small switch has been for our clients. Many of them find that thinking about their milestones as Lanterns instead of goals opens the door to more fun and creative ways of working toward them. That's also why we're using the imagery of the night hike, to illustrate that all meaningful achievements on your path create more light as you make progress up the mountain.

A Lantern has three main characteristics. First, it is a distinct achievement. Second, it's a stepping stone toward something bigger. And third, it opens new possibilities for yourself and others.

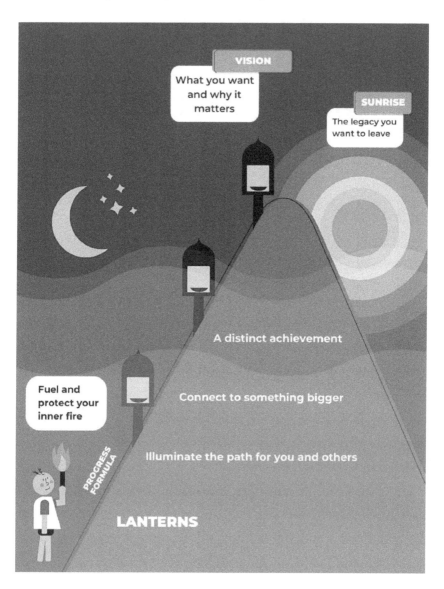

Put together, these three features are what differentiate Lanterns from the average goal and keep you from getting lost in the Goal Swamp. It's hard to know if you're making progress when you don't have a specific target to aim for. That's why the first quality of a good Lantern is that it's a distinct achievement.

A Lantern Is a Distinct Achievement

My favorite picture of David Meerman Scott shows him midair, in his swimsuit with glaciers in the background, about to plunge into the Antarctic Ocean. Taken in 2014, this picture captures this best-selling author and internationally celebrated business speaker looking vibrant and incredibly fit. But just a few years prior he was in a very different state.

Right before his fiftieth birthday, David went to visit his doctor for a checkup and the news wasn't good. His doctor suggested medication to keep some health issues at bay and David wasn't happy about it. This wakeup call was amplified by the fact that two of his close friends had passed away suddenly due to their own health issues shortly before.

So, on David's fiftieth birthday, looking at himself in the mirror and seeing the naked truth, he decided it was time to get healthy. And while many people have the wish to get healthy, David chose a few distinct Lanterns to work toward.

One was being able to do a pull-up.

"Prior to then I couldn't do any pull-ups," David told us. "I literally could not do one."

What helped David's intention get results rather than land in the pile of forgotten wishes was that he focused his attention on something specific. Just as a physical lantern gives off light and heat, a Lantern moment in your life is when you have completed a tangible activity. It could be the first thousand dollars made in your business or buying your dream home.

Making it distinct means you can't argue if it happened or not. If your Lantern is something vaguer, such as "to have more energy" or a "better relationship," you will have a hard time noticing when you've reached it. Being able to acknowledge and even celebrate something is part of what makes lighting a Lantern so powerful. As humans, if we don't feel like we're making progress it's hard to stay motivated.

> **As humans, if we don't feel like we're making progress it's hard to stay motivated.**

Setting a destination that allows you to arrive and say, "Yes, I did it!" makes all the difference for maintaining momentum on your journey.

A Lantern Connects to Something Bigger

Once David committed to his Lantern of being able to do a single pull-up as part of his greater desire to have a healthy life, things moved quickly. He changed his diet, brought himself to a weight he was happy about, and established an exercise routine that helped him light the Lantern. Now in his early sixties, he can do not just one pull-up but sixty in a single workout.

David's Lantern gave him a milestone to focus on that helped him make measurable and consistent progress toward something bigger: his overall picture of health. While the pull-up was a notable achievement, all the habits he created to get there had the additional effect of enhancing his professional life. These benefits to what mattered deeply to him helped David stay on track despite how hard the path was.

Let's consider a common objective for business owners and leaders: the revenue milestone. Revenue goals can be great Lanterns since they're distinct and clear. It's hard to argue with a dollar number in your bank account. But unless that achievement is directly connected with the bigger dream you have for your life, it won't serve the full function of a Lantern. That's because revenue by itself does not connect to your deeper purpose. Revenue is a number that reflects the value you created in the world but it doesn't touch the essence of why you are here in the first place.

While Lanterns must be specific about *what* you're looking to achieve, *why* that achievement matters to you is even more important. Let's say you want to create a company that has a big impact in the world and where people can do their best work. While that speaks to a bigger purpose it isn't yet a distinct Lantern.

> **Revenue is a number that reflects the value you created in the world but it doesn't touch the essence of why you are here in the first place.**

Getting more distinct, you could say that the Lantern is to reach ten million dollars in revenue, and for your company to be in a place where your employees thrive and grow. You could go a layer deeper and say that you want an eNPS (employee net promoter score) of +50, to reflect your commitment to the well-being of your employees.

Now, if the way you reach that ten million—the first part of your Lantern—is through seeding toxic competition between sales reps, yelling at your team for missing targets, or any other management techniques from *Glengarry Glen Ross*, you may hit the revenue target but you'll miss the Lantern. Coffee should be for everyone, not just closers.

If your dream is to truly have a supportive culture in your business, the Lantern will not be lit until you've figured out how to reach the revenue milestone in a work environment that people feel proud of having created.

A Lantern Opens New Possibilities for Yourself and Others

David Meerman Scott is one of my favorite examples of someone who is Superabounding in many areas of life. He is the author of thirteen books, one of which, *The New Rules of Marketing and PR*, has sold nearly half a million copies and is published in thirty languages from Arabic to Vietnamese. His writing, speaking, and coaching work has impacted countless businesses around the world, including ours.

There's no question that David's Lantern, to do one pull-up, helped him become healthier and had a ripple effect on everyone around him. The pull-up wasn't the purpose, it was the catalyst. All the work it took to get to that point had physiological effects that now support him as he appears onstage, travels, writes, and coaches. Not to mention the positive mindset shift that inevitably comes from seeing oneself as vibrant, healthy, and capable of making a big life change.

A Lantern isn't the final ascent up the mountain. It is the light that illuminates a multitude of paths you couldn't see before and becomes a beacon for people on the trail behind you.

"Being that much healthier has helped me to be a more effective speaker and has made me better at pretty much everything I do," David said.

And in his mid-sixties he's not retired. In fact, he's inspiring more people through his work than others would even dream of in their thirties and forties. Not to mention other sixty-somethings who can use his story as inspiration for their own progress, in work and in life.

A Lantern isn't the final ascent up the mountain. It is the light that illuminates a multitude of paths you couldn't see before and becomes a beacon for people on the trail behind you. Next, we're

going to teach you the tool that has helped countless entrepreneurs and leaders light the Lanterns along the path to their most important dreams—all by learning how to make consistent progress.

Your Plan

The cold night is upon you now. The mountain somehow looks twice as big as it did in the daylight hours and for a moment you think about settling in for the night and calling a cab back to town in the morning.

You remember the first serious conversation you had with your climbing coach about this journey:

"Everyone has a moment right before they begin that they almost quit. Just remember, that is the first challenge you will face. You can't fully commit to climbing your mountain until it is looming above you. Deciding to start is the first obstacle of many, and that is why we train for this."

Her words wash over you and you remind yourself of what she taught you.

"There are only three things between you and the top of the mountain:

"First, you have to make sure you are only taking what is necessary. Most people bring a whole bunch of excess crap they don't need on the mountain, and that's a mistake. It makes the whole trek harder and heavier than necessary, so only carry things that are going to help you. Leave the extra baggage at home.

"The next thing between you and the top is the actual terrain and the challenging obstacles between each lantern. Your training will condition you to be as ready as possible to deal with this.

"Finally, and most importantly, there is your reason for attempting the climb. If that reason isn't big enough to hold all the struggles along the way, you won't make it."

You close your eyes and connect to your breathing, just like your coach taught you. You might not feel ready, but in that moment you commit. This is your mountain to climb.

CHAPTER 5

Following the Progress Formula

By Steve

Erin and I developed the Progress Formula after years of banging our heads against the wall trying to work within the constraints of tedious or complicated business and goal-setting frameworks. We wanted an easy-to-explain tool that would help our clients make progress, but wasn't so complicated it would take a 500-page manual to understand and use in their life. Most importantly, it had to acknowledge that success can be hard and unpredictable, without letting people waste away in self-limiting beliefs.

If you think of your life as a night hike, your Vision is the top of the mountain you are determined to climb. There are many paths to the summit but there are just as many ways to wander aimlessly around the bottom, breathing the noxious vapors of the Goal Swamp.

A clarified Vision is your guide to making more aligned decisions and organizing your life around something meaningful to you. Your Vision will keep you on a path that's moving you toward the top, not going in circles thinking you're getting somewhere.

But if all it took to get there was just putting one foot in front of the other, everyone would be basking in the glory of their fully realized Vision right now. The first thing that gets in the way and slows most people down is that they carry a heavy backpack filled with things that aren't all that useful to their climb. This is called Static.

Going on a night hike up a mountain is already hard. It's no place for things that don't belong on the trip. Static is the mental chatter and strong emotions that make the very real challenges in front of you harder than they need to be. Being in a Static state is like carrying things you can't use and don't need for the hike instead of food, proper gear, and water. And while you may read that and think you would never be so foolish, this is the trick of Static at play. Your Static feels real to you and that is why you don't notice it. Your inner world of beliefs about yourself and your life has the power to lift you up or weigh you down, and soon we will teach you how to spot the Static beliefs that stall your progress so you can stop making the terrain feel harder than needed.

If Static represents the inner landscape of unhelpful beliefs and emotions that make your night hike harder, Challenges represent the outer terrain. In the Progress Formula, Challenges are the actual territory and obstacles between you and your Vision. On the mountain of your Vision you will deal with Static and Challenges all the time, so it pays to know which is which and what they look like for you. And they're not always dramatic, but they will slow you down.

One fine Monday morning, Erin and I were looking at our calendars when she said, "I'm feeling so overwhelmed right now. I don't know what to do." She walked away and got ready for her first coaching call of the day, which was coming up soon. When I saw her an hour later, everything had changed. She was a force of nature, not only adjusting her calendar for maximum output for the week but cracking jokes, coming up with ideas for podcasts, and generally acting like the boss she is.

"What happened?" I asked.

"When I sat down to coach this morning, I remembered how much I love doing this and how helpful our work is in people's lives," she said. In other words, she was no longer consumed by her Static. She had tuned in to the Vision of the business, which helped her prioritize the week and move forward. A simple shift in her attention resulted in a completely different outcome for the day.

To be clear, the answer is not, "*Think positively and all your problems will be solved.*" Static needs to be respected and managed with care, since it's part of you. We will cover this in more detail in a later chapter. But the example with Erin illustrates what a powerful role our inner state plays in our ability to move forward.

For my fellow logic geeks, there's actually a formula to make consistent, healthy progress. It looks like this: if (Vision > (Static × Challenges)) then Progress. If your Vision is greater than the product of your Static times your Challenges, you will make progress.

> If (**Vision** > (**Static** × **Challenges**)) then **Progress.**

It shows that you have three levers in your life for moving toward your next Lantern. First, you can strengthen your Vision, which we will explore in depth in the next chapter. Vision is the starting point, because if you don't have a reason for going somewhere or you don't know where it is you want to go, you're likely wandering around the Goal Swamp at best. Everything begins with Vision.

In our company, we start every meeting talking about our Vision and we do our best to ensure that every decision we make and client we work with is aligned with it. Tuning in to your Vision tips the odds of progress in your favor because it helps you remember why you're making the effort. That's why Vision comes first in the Progress Formula and stands alone.

> **The Progress Formula is most useful when you have a Lantern you want to light that seems bigger than the capacity you currently have.**

What follows are the only two things between you and your next Lantern: Static and Challenges. That's it. It's some combination of both of those. The Progress Formula will help you quiet the inner voices of doubt, fear, or self-criticism (your Static) and accomplish the necessary tasks on the path (your Challenges).

Once you learn it and start to apply its principles, you can use it to Superabound in any area of your life. The Progress Formula is most useful when you have a Lantern you want to light that seems bigger than the capacity you currently have. It will help you overcome Challenges and make a distant-seeming dream possible.

You can see that the backpack of Static gets heavier the more it fills with unhelpful thoughts and beliefs, making the rolling hills in front of us feel more like towering mountains. But if we can fuel ourselves with Vision, clear out our Static, and shrink the Challenges ahead into manageable chunks, our progress becomes inevitable. Eventually we find ourselves like the character up top: with a fuller heart and the metaphorical balloons and rainbows that celebrate the movement toward our Vision.

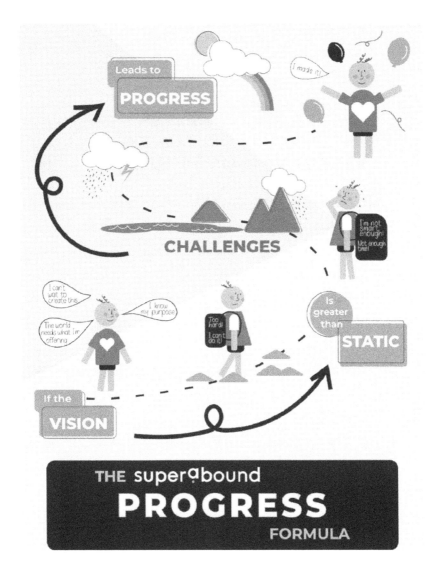

The Progress Formula is what helps you take what would otherwise just be wishes and turn them into meaningful actions. We're going to return to it throughout the book so that it becomes a natural tool for you and a lens through which you see the world and your work. But let's begin with the engine for your progress in the world: Vision.

Vision versus Mountain

It is decided. You are doing this climb. Your resolve mingles in your belly with bone melting fear. You look down to see your hands are shaking and can hear your heart pounding in your ears. But deep down you already know that the resolve will win out.

"It makes sense to feel scared. This is a big thing I am attempting and it matters to me a lot. It would be strange if I felt calm right now," you say to yourself reassuringly.

You sit down and continue to breathe deeply, allowing your body a chance to process the decision to go. You pull out your small notebook and open it to the first page.

You look down at your own careful handwriting from a few weeks ago where you wrote a short note to yourself about your Vision and your reasons for the night hike on this mountain. You read the words and feel so grateful to your past self for knowing you would need some bolstering in these final moments before your journey begins.

After a few moments you notice your breathing has returned to normal and your heartbeat is not drowning out the sounds of the night any longer.

You shut the book and listen. In the direction of the mountain an owl hoots as if to beckon you to begin and you feel a smile break across your face.

"I am on my way," you say softly.

CHAPTER 6

Discovering Your Superabound Vision

By Steve

Tapping Out to Tap In

"I can't do it. I don't want to do it anymore. I'm tapping out."

Even though she only had one more year before getting her math and business degrees, Lenore Johnson took a leap and left the corporate career track behind. She was finally ready to take her father's advice.

He told me all the time, "You don't need to work for anyone else. Whatever you do, either do it for yourself or be in charge," Lenore shared with Erin and me as we sat in LenJo Bakes, her shop in Kitchener, Ontario. That advice from her father during her youth had made an impression, as evidenced by the portmanteau of her name on the door.

Lenore excused herself to get up and greet one of her regular customers, and I took a moment to enjoy the notes of ginger, chocolate, cinnamon, and butter mixing in the air. Music played while people worked and the plants along the walls gave life to the space that features rows of baked goods.

This is one element of Lenore Johnson's Vision in action. She created a friendly, relaxed space that is home to some of the finest baking in the world (think flavor combos like white chocolate cranberry pistachio fudge). And even though she's on the mountain climbing toward her big Vision now, it took her a while to get here and the path has been anything but straightforward.

Lenore had a love for baking at an early age, both with the homemade cookies and Rice Krispie treats her mother made, as well as her passion for the Food Network. Over spring break, she would watch the network's cake competition shows for hours a day, including the reruns she had just seen. Lenore dreamed to someday be able to do it just as well as the folks on TV.

But even with the advice from her father to start her own business and her devotion to baking, she still felt the pull to follow the same blueprint as most others around her. That's because, deep down, she didn't believe it was possible to build a life by running a bakery. So, she studied at a top university and secured coveted internships with big companies. That's where she discovered that the conventional path gave her neither satisfaction nor a sense that she was in the right place.

At one internship with a prominent retailer, she was given a project that her boss expected to take four months. She finished it in two and had found herself with nothing to do for two more months. The rest of the time she tapped away at a keyboard, doing, as Lenore told us, "literally nothing, speaking to no one, and being exhausted at the end of the day."

She spent another term doing meaningful work in the public sector until her supervisors went on an extended strike and she was stuck, again, with nothing creative to devote her brain power to. Lenore's decision to choose her Vision and climb her own mountain came during a programming job for a well-known clothing store.

Despite being successful within the company, she realized that what made her tick was true connection with other humans. "I still just came to work, said hello to people for three or four minutes, sat down at a computer, said hello for ten minutes during lunch, did a puzzle, then worked for the rest of my day before commuting back home."

Beyond the fact that Lenore wasn't feeling connected, she questioned the impact she was having as the scope of her decisions was choosing colors for displays. So, with one more year of university to go, she left her corporate Goal Swamp and set out to find a meaningful mountain to climb. She had tried the path of following the world's expectations for how to earn a living and found it wasn't right for her.

She took a leap and enrolled in baking school, which unlocked an opportunity to live and study as a pastry chef in France. It was there that she discovered the French reverence for food. "You can look at a pound of butter and just say, 'Yeah, cool, butter,'" she said, "But actually, there's a dairy farmer, and a cow, and somebody to make the butter and then somebody had to drive it to you. When you pick an apple off a stack in the store, do you know how long those trees have been planted before they were fruiting and how many times they've been pruned and which ones have been selected to be the best yielding, best tasting, longest lasting? It's work."

After her time in France, she continued her culinary journey in a Michelin-starred restaurant in England. A silent kitchen, as most restaurants at that level are. No music. No chitchat. Not Lenore's vibe either.

In England she discovered her passion for making cakes but found it difficult to break out of her previous role as a pastry chef and *just* focus on cakes. So, when a friend invited Lenore to join her at a winery restaurant in Waiheke Island, New Zealand, to make wedding cakes, Lenore packed up and moved to the other side of the world.

This was a milestone moment. She finally had the role she was looking for, and in a beautiful location, but there was another Lantern ahead to light. Thankfully she had a manager who knew Lenore wanted to own her own business one day and encouraged her to take that next step.

"I'm not paying you enough here for what you're doing," her boss told her one day. Up to that point, Lenore was being paid by the hour to manage the entire cake making process from initial consultation, ordering all supplies, creating and delivering the cake, while the winery enjoyed the full profit from the sale. "I'm the middleman and I'm taking much of your potential money," her boss said. "I'm not helping you anyway, so you might as well go out and do this on your own."

So, Lenore rented a kitchen near the winery, bought a mixer, and posted a digital flyer on Facebook and Instagram announcing her new business. Within two weeks she was making cakes for people's weddings, retirements, anniversaries, and other special occasions. Lenore was well on the way up the mountain of her true Vision. She was baking cakes, working directly with people during important moments in their lives, and running her own business. These were all important Lanterns.

But the next Lantern ahead was a big, yet critical, one: creating community.

"I just wanted a place that people could come and feel like they're a part of it. I wanted to inject this feeling of true community, where someone knows what you like to order and what's going on in your life. You're not just shopping for shopping's sake," said Lenore. She decided to evolve beyond the pop-up cake shop and open a storefront.

Her hometown of Kitchener, Ontario, was always close to her heart, so she packed up again, moved back home, and opened her own shop. When you've got a good thing going, moving across the world to start a business from scratch is fraught with challenges. Not to mention LenJo Bakes opened its doors mere weeks before COVID-19 lockdowns began in 2020. Imagine owning a business where a major part of your revenue comes from baking wedding cakes while all weddings are canceled or drastically downsized. It was a hard few years to say the least.

However, the Lantern was lit and she now runs her own store. Her Vision continues to evolve as well. Drawing from her love of people and community, she is committed to creating an environment in the food industry where people can thrive and enjoy their work. "Most kitchens are incredibly toxic," said Lenore, "because most chefs fear being usurped. But that's not me, I don't care. My bakers come in with lists of what they want to make and what they want Valentine's Day to look like, for instance. I want to set people up for their own success, where we can all grow together."

That's what makes LenJo Bakes such a special place. You feel it in the vibe, and you taste it in the food. But had she not pursued her own path and instead been satisfied with what the world says a successful career should look like, her business wouldn't have existed.

And, true to her childhood dreams, she even appeared on TV as a judge on Canada's *Wall of Bakers*, inspiring the next generation of pastry chefs.

Discovering Your Superabound Vision

Most people live life from day to day, never questioning their purpose or how big their contribution to the world could be.

When you decide to Superabound, your life will start to feel abundant because your daily activities will be in alignment with your top of the mountain Vision. One of the most important things you need to do first is clearly articulate your Vision so you know exactly what you are working toward and why it matters to you.

Most people live life from day to day, never questioning their purpose or how big their contribution to the world could be.

A lot of people skip over this part of the process either because they think they already have their Vision locked in and fear what evolving or changing it might mean. Or they believe it is spiritual-sounding busy work and would rather lace up their boots and hike the mountain in front of them.

Whether or not you fall into either of these camps, we urge you to stick with us for a few pages to learn why the Superabound Vision approach is essential to the rest of this book being useful to you on your journey.

Your Vision is not just the uppermost peak on your mountain, it is the compass to help you find your way there. Rather than a final destination, we've found it's more helpful to think of it as a practice.

As such, time spent reflecting on and clarifying your Vision strengthens its presence in your life and gives it more power to shape the world around you. Return to this chapter regularly, at least once a year, for inspiration and clarity on this point.

A Superabound Vision consists of three elements. It:

- Transcends any particular path or accomplishment

- Expresses your potential

- Is fulfilled in part with each milestone

Let's explore each of these in more depth.

Vision Transcends Any Path or Accomplishment

Vision is an overarching umbrella of purpose, not any particular achievement. It's the underlying motivator for choosing the mountain you want to climb. Because once you know the mountain, there are multiple paths that lead to the summit. This is what allows you to continue to pursue your Vision even as your interests and life circumstances change.

For instance, my first career was in classical music playing trumpet. I thought that my Vision was to be the world's greatest trumpeter, playing principal in the Chicago Symphony, my hometown band. However, this turned out to be one of the many possible Lanterns on the mountain, not my Vision itself.

My first full-time job as a trumpeter was with the US Navy Band in Washington, DC. It was one of the best military bands in the world, and I played at high-profile events including presidential inaugurations and funerals. There's nothing a musician's ego loves more than knowing that their show was seen by millions of people.

My skills as a trumpeter were blossoming as well, as I gained the confidence that only comes from being a full-time professional surrounded by great players. I was on my way to lighting that Lantern of playing in the Chicago Symphony or another top orchestra.

But something else started to emerge. I began to discover a passion for spirituality at this same time and had found a community that felt like home. I would take leave from the band to attend extended meditation retreats in faraway places such as Italy and India, and closer ones in the Berkshire mountains of western Massachusetts.

I pursued a master's degree in conscious evolution (yes, that is a thing) and dove deep into the mysteries of life and the Universe. The friends I made on the spiritual path were the ones I felt most compelled to spend time with. We started cooking up ideas for businesses we could build that would allow us to create wealth and freedom so we could have an even bigger impact with our spiritual interests.

I was torn between my old definition of success as a musician and my new Vision of what could be possible in my life. So, I made a decision: I would follow the path of consciousness and entrepreneurship wherever it led, even though it meant leaving behind a Lantern so significant that it had felt like a life's calling.

That decision had big consequences.

I got divorced, sold my house, and gave away most of my musical library (but kept a few horns, just in case). I didn't reenlist in the band when my term of service was up. My friends were terrified that I was joining a cult and ruining my life. And from a certain perspective they were right. My old life was crumbling.

But what supported me was my confidence in a Superabound Vision that was taking shape. I was seeing that what motivated me was the pursuit of beauty and creativity itself. It wasn't just music that

I loved, and following this realization allowed me to change what I considered success to be and to embrace a bigger Vision for my life.

If I had remained tied to my Lantern of getting a prestigious orchestra job, I wouldn't have realized that what mattered most to me was helping people realize the life the Universe is dreaming for them. I wouldn't have allowed myself to explore other paths. And I would have missed out on a decade of alternative life experience in a spiritual community (where Erin and I met), as well as the ensuing adventures in high-growth start-ups and now in coaching.

But because I allowed myself to embrace a Superabound Vision that transcended the unlit Lanterns of my youth, I was able to choose a path other than that of a classical musician. Life itself became my canvas for self-expression and exploration. And allowing myself to explore while remaining true to what matters to me has brought so much fulfillment.

That's what I hope this insight unlocks for you—allowing the expression of your life's purpose to take different forms while staying true to what matters most. One of the most important parts of discovering your own transcendent Vision is disentangling what you want from what others say you should want.

One clue you might be tangled in the weeds of the Goal Swamp and need to find a more authentic mountain to climb is if you find yourself wishing your life looked fundamentally different in some way. If you dread your work or the structure of your daily schedule, you might be on the wrong path, or on the wrong mountain altogether.

Even a path like entrepreneurship, which requires tremendous personal drive, could still be someone else's dream for you rather than your own. If you grew up being trained to take over the family business, then running a company is celebrated, but only in that very narrow scope. I know someone who inherited their family business and, while outwardly he was very successful, he struggled with the pressure and demands of being the figurehead of the company while his true passion was in his artistic pursuits. Discovering and following his Superabound Vision earlier in life might have prevented years of unwanted stress.

Knowing that you can fulfill your Vision even if you change directions will open new possibilities in your life and free you from unhelpful assumptions about what you "should" be doing.

Vision Expresses Your Potential

A Superabound Vision is one that requires you to grow.

In working with thousands of people across different backgrounds and industries, one thing I've noticed in those who Superabound is that they crave growth. They want to actualize their potential in service of their bigger vision. You may have potential and talent, but a worthy Vision requires you to activate them and develop capacities you don't yet have today. And you can't know exactly what they will be from where you are on the mountain.

A Superabound Vision is one that requires you to grow.

You can't grow simply by thinking about it or from training exercises that are disconnected from reality. Real growth only happens from taking on the Challenges on the path to your Vision.

It is easy to sit on your comfortable couch and read someone else's account of what it is like to hike up a mountain at night, but you'll only know just how dark and scary the forest can get when you're there. It is only when you're putting one foot in front of the other with nothing but the light of a torch to guide you that you will discover what it takes to keep moving forward.

This is a holistic and healthy way of approaching growth, one where you acclimate to the demands of your Superabound Vision as you go. That doesn't mean it is fun or easy. Much of the time, growth only happens as a response to failure and needing to find another way around the obstacle in front of you.

On the metaphorical night hike, this acclamation looks like your muscles recovering from the exertion and the cramps, allowing you to become stronger, your feet healing from the blisters and becoming tougher so you can set a new pace appropriate for the environment that you're in. Acclimation is only possible while you're *in the process*.

That's the reason high-altitude climbers spend time at base camp before going up, or elite athletes devote themselves to preseason training.

The Superabound approach to Vision and growth makes you more resilient to the Challenges of the path ahead. A new business owner having a proposal rejected might feel like their company is destined to fail. They may not have any meetings on the books and think this is the end. Whereas a business owner who has already had one hundred proposals rejected is better able to learn from that experience, reframe it as a step closer to their next win, and not waste time rehashing it or letting the rejection stall forward movement.

So even though the pain may be the same, the more seasoned entrepreneur will have the internal resilience to handle their emotions without a lot of drama. And a Superabound business owner is likely to use the rejection as a creative spark to make their sales process better.

Another way to think about activating your potential is to see it as becoming more of yourself. This is different from becoming more of who you think you should be, or more like your favorite superstar. The world doesn't need you to be LeBron James. LeBron's doing a great job at it already.

Often when people think about growth they are starting from a place of lack, or somehow feeling not good enough. Convinced they are flawed in some fundamental way, they set out to become someone new—usually someone their culture said they should be more like.

Hang out with members of any niche community and you'll notice the pull to be more like the heroes of that group. Silicon Valley entrepreneurs? They're all fired up about their next funding round, joint venture, or product release—sounding more like Steve Jobs than like the quirky individuals they actually are. Life coaches? They're often giving off more Tony Robbins or Martha Beck vibes and catch-phrases than what's actually going on in their hearts and minds.

And it makes sense. Because if someone else has figured out how to be successful in their field, then it is easy to believe that becoming more like them will bring you a similar result.

The problem is that mimicking a superstar cuts you off from discovering your own path and potential.

I'm not saying don't learn from people who have already done what you're looking to do. I have stacks of books by people I admire on my nightstand and audiobooks in my ear as I move through the day. But learning for the sake of copying someone's formula is dis-empowering to you and usually stems from a lack of belief in your own capacity for success. By contrast, learning from others with the intention of getting inspired by what is aligned with your wisdom is when you stop acting like a cardboard cutout of your hero and become the superstar only you could be.

The kind of growth that fuels a Superabound Vision worthy of your lifetime pursuit is one that expresses your potential. Rather than squishing yourself into the mold of your culture's heroes and wondering why you aren't as successful as they are, ask yourself: *"In what ways do I want to develop? What growth would delight me and bring me closer to my Vision?"*

Think of your interests, passions, and intuitive hits as seeds within you. Expressing your potential means paying attention to those seeds and helping them grow in service of your larger Vision.

We have a client that we've worked with for years whose Vision is to help women succeed in her traditionally male-dominated industry. This is a Superabound Vision because it transcends any path or accomplishment she could have. It requires her to express her full potential as a leader, and each achievement along the way fulfills her larger purpose to some degree.

One Lantern she needs to light is becoming a lead decision-maker at her organization so she can change the culture to one that values equality and ends gender bias. This already brilliant person will have to become a beginner of sorts and gain brand-new skills. At some point she may have to tap out of the prestigious projects that she's involved with in order to tap in to her role as a high-level leader. To set herself up for this opportunity she is investing in her own leadership and mindset development.

By relying on her intrinsic motivation to grow, she is making big leaps toward her Lantern and ultimately to her Superabound Vision.

Unfortunately, this is not the way most people approach growth on the path to greatness. Far too often, people see their gaps as reasons to berate or doubt themselves, as though they shouldn't have any weaknesses.

The journey toward a Superabound Vision is hard. Don't make it harder by being a jerk to yourself.

But if this is your story, here is a reality check: The journey toward a Superabound Vision is hard. Don't make it harder by being a jerk to yourself.

Approaching growth with warmth allows your path to be fulfilling with every step. If you are able to move forward with self-love, the acclimation you experience will be much more sustainable than if you're "kicking your own ass," "pushing yourself," "crushing your targets," or any other of the thousands of sayings that contain a certain measure of violence within them.

And the only reason for this extremely common view of growth requiring a level of self-scolding is because our metaphors haven't caught up with our understanding of how human brains work. We're learning more every day that intrinsic motivators like curiosity and play help us perform better than extrinsic ones like financial reward and competition.

> **It's no wonder why so many people feel empty after they achieve a goal. They've been cutting out so many parts of themselves along the way that there's not much of them left when they arrive.**

We achieve our greater potentials when we feel safe and are seen as inherently whole rather than when we feel alone and have something to prove. (Side note: Just by being here and reading this book you're already engaged in a process that has self-warmth at its heart. We hope you'll feel this firsthand as you go deeper in the book.) Yet, we so often attempt to grow through an adversarial and even destructive view of the world.

It's no wonder why so many people feel empty after they achieve a goal. They've been cutting out so many parts of themselves along the way that there's not much of them left when they arrive.

A Superabound Vision requires growth. After all, if you didn't need to grow, you'd be living your dreams already. You would have all the skills, resources, and the mindset required to be enjoying life at the finish line. Growth is a must for a worthy Vision. But until you're able to download skills like Neo did with kung fu in *The Matrix*, the way to Superabound is to summon the untapped resources within you.

Each Milestone Fulfills the Vision in Part

An unfulfilling Vision is one that requires you to achieve it in full to be satisfied. This is the world where so many people live, always chasing the carrot that moves just as fast as they do. Living this way, you never get to taste the sweetness of victory because nothing you achieve will suffice until you reach the end (which you may not see in your lifetime if your Vision is big enough).

The solution to this torturous, never-ending game of chase is to have a Vision where each milestone toward it contains the essence of the whole thing. A Superabound Vision is like a hologram in this sense. Holograms are created by projecting an image from two different light sources onto a photographic plate. Shine a single light source onto that plate and the hologram appears. The amazing thing is that if you break the plate into a hundred pieces, every single one of them contains the entire image, just a smaller, slightly fuzzier version of it.

A Superabound Vision worth dedicating your life to is one in which every small achievement is much like that holographic plate. Each achievement casts an image of what it is you're creating, albeit a little smaller than what you have in mind. Unlike a hologram, however, instead of losing its clarity, each smaller achievement strengthens and brings your Superabound Vision into focus.

But there's a strong belief in our culture that opposes the idea that smaller achievements deserve any fanfare. Many people think that if they congratulate themselves too soon or celebrate Lanterns on the way up the mountain they'll lose their edge, become complacent, and won't continue making progress toward their ultimate Vision. They believe in withholding satisfaction until they've reached the end. But this aggressive approach doesn't work for most people.

A few years ago, I decided to light a Lantern that might seem unrelated to my Vision of helping people realize the life the Universe is dreaming for them: cycling up Haleakalā, the 10,000-foot volcano on the island of Maui. What made this a real Lantern rather than just a random adventure was that I had zero road biking experience at the point when I decided to light it. With our next trip to Hawaii booked five months in the future, attempting this ride was a big challenge for me and one I hoped might inspire others.

It was an ambitious idea. I had never biked for six consecutive hours before—let alone up a mountain. It was going to take months of training while managing a full-time career, raising two young kids, and, here's the tricky part, not adding more to Erin's plate as she was building her company. But despite all the inner chatter and outer challenges that told me I couldn't or shouldn't cycle up the volcano, I started training on our indoor bike, getting mindset coaching and physiotherapy to support me along the way.

When the day of the ride finally arrived, I was nervous and excited, still having never done any real road biking. But I had my plan in place: I would bike at an easy pace and stop every few thousand feet of elevation to celebrate my progress, rest, and take in the view.

I was tempted to keep up with others in my group and race to the top as fast as possible. I could have berated myself when my legs started to burn and pushed on instead of taking needed rest. Instead, I followed my plan.

At 2,000 feet above sea level, I was surrounded by lush tropical plants. By 4,000 feet the tropical growth had given way to grasslands, with an even greater view of the surrounding island. Around 5,000 feet the path was lined with fragrant eucalyptus trees and mist. At 7,000 feet it was pure sunshine, deep valleys, and desert grasses. Then at 9,000 feet it became cold and rocky, looking more like the surface of the moon than a tropical island. But I was on the home stretch.

The final ascent to 10,000 feet was both brutal and exhilarating. With each pedal stroke up this ridiculously steep climb my legs threatened to quit. My lungs burned in the thin air but I somehow made it up the hill to the final outlook. I was greeted with mystical views of the volcano's crater and the neighboring islands in the distance. My Lantern was lit, not through brute force but with thoughtful connection to my Vision. It also included a willingness to meet the challenges of doing the work before me day after day from the moment I had this wild idea of standing at the top of a volcano in the middle of the ocean.

If I would have approached this ride the way many people approach their Vision, I would have missed the magic of the changing ecosystem along the way. First, there is no way I would have made it to the top if I hadn't taken breaks and let my body rest. But if it were possible to have made it without any pauses or appreciation, I would have certainly missed out on the delightful conversations to be had with my fellow riders and all the other small moments of joy along the way. My experience of the ride would have been a hard climb to the top with a fleeting moment of relief before heading back down, cold, emotionally empty, and exhausted.

Instead, I celebrated my progress throughout and the extraordinary experiences at each point all the way to the top.

Haleakalā was one Lantern lit on the path to my Superabound Vision. When I feel like there is something I want to do, I have that experience in my pocket to remind me that we humans are capable of amazing things if we decide they are important enough to us. I've shared this story with many people who believed it was too late for them to light a particular Lantern. If a forty-three-year-old casual cyclist can bike up a volcano with a few months of training on an indoor bike, maybe their own Lantern isn't so far-fetched.

Your Vision Might Outlive You

If you have a Superabound Vision, chances are it will be so big and so complex you may not see it fully realized in your lifetime. Demanding that you achieve your Vision in full to acknowledge your accomplishment and worthiness will do one of two things: either you will shrink your Vision so you don't have to suffer that lack of acknowledgment, or you will live with a sense of emptiness even amid outward success. This is another reason we celebrate the Lanterns lit and every milestone along the way.

> **Demanding that you achieve your Vision in full to acknowledge your accomplishment and worthiness will do one of two things: either you will shrink your Vision so you don't have to suffer that lack of acknowledgment, or you will live with a sense of emptiness even amid outward success.**

Many people resist this idea. They worry that celebrating small steps will be demotivating and that they won't achieve greatness if they show grace and warmth to themselves along the way. I have found the opposite to be true. Acknowledging how far you've come is one of the most powerful sources of inspiration. Look at a child's face when they write their name for the first time. Pure delight. They aren't waiting until they get a PhD to be in awe of their growth and learning. Rather than slowing them down, attaining this new capacity and proudly declaring "I DID IT" only fuels their belief in themselves. Each step and each Lantern lit is the prize, not just the diploma at the end of the path.

But at some point, many of us shift out of this childlike joy of discovery for its own sake, where each win is as good as the end goal, and deny ourselves the pleasure of progress. This is how many people find themselves in the Goal Swamp, muddy and discouraged. They are not living and reveling in the present moment, but rather aching for a future outcome they hope will make them feel whole.

Instead, when you embrace the small wins baked into the process, you increase your opportunities to create deeper connections with yourself and others. One conversation I would have missed had I been focused on breaking the land speed record up Haleakalā has stayed with me.

My tour group had stopped around 3,500 feet for a drink and snack break when I struck up a conversation with a fellow cyclist who worked as a radiologist in New York City. He looked me right in the eyes as he said, "It's crazy that we're out here. We both have little kids and partners who will watch them so we can do this thing. But you know what, every single day at work I tell people that the life they had thought they would be living is not to be." He leaned in and said, "*Carpe diem*, my friend. Live your dream today because you are never guaranteed tomorrow."

> **Each day, each decision, where you are in alignment with your Vision is your Vision in action.**

Each day, each decision, where you are in alignment with your Vision is your Vision in action. You are bringing something that only used to live in your imagination into the world. And while you may not live to see the fullness of your Vision realized, you can go to sleep every night satisfied knowing you are living in alignment with what matters most to you.

YOUR TURN

- What is your Superabound Vision that transcends any particular accomplishment?

- How does dedicating yourself to this Vision express your potential?

- What is the next Lantern you are going to light toward that Vision?

- How are you living your Vision and celebrating each Lantern lit?

If you would like our support crafting your Vision, join the Superabound Collective at *beSuperabound.com/collective* to learn the process we use with our community.

Take Only What You Need

You check your backpack one more time to see if you have everything for your climb.

You lay out your gear. Water? Check. Food? Check. Extra socks? Check. Journal to take notes in? Check.

But as you get deeper into your bag you find swimming goggles stuffed in a side pouch. Your favorite toy truck from when you were five. A small but heavy sculpture your first love made you for your birthday, only to break up with you the next week. And a stein from your trip to Germany that you forgot to wash and now reeks of old beer. Yuck.

All this stuff has been taking up space in your pack without you even knowing it, potentially weighing you down at a time when you need to be as unencumbered as possible to deal with the tough terrain ahead.

"Good thing I checked," you think, grateful you took the time to remove the things that won't help you on this trip instead of bolting up the mountain with extra, unhelpful baggage.

You stand up and put your backpack on, feeling relieved at its comfortable new weight and fresher scent, knowing you're now only carrying exactly what you need.

CHAPTER 7

H.E.A.L.ing the Static

By Erin

Static Beliefs

A few years ago, before Steve joined me full time in our coaching business, I witnessed him experience several months in a high Static state. He had been excelling in his corporate work and when it came time for a new manager to be chosen for his team, he was promoted to the role. Almost immediately, the size of his team doubled, then tripled. Like many new managers, he found himself quickly shuttled from doing work he was an expert at to doing something he had never done before at this level: managing people.

If you couldn't tell from reading this book so far, Steve loves people. He is a natural cheerleader, inherently positive and trusting. But at this time in his career, he wasn't a master coach and hadn't received any training or mentorship on how do his new job as a "People Lead."

The next part of this story will sound sickeningly familiar to anyone who has been jettisoned out of their role as an individual contributor into the nebulous world of management (or entrepreneurship). Over the course of a few months I watched my joyful, confident partner turn into a reserved, self-doubting whisper of his former self.

His mind seemed to be only on work, and he could talk about nothing else. It didn't matter if we were at a party, watching a movie at home, or out for a lovely dinner, the conversation would always turn to a struggle with someone on his team or a tricky deal with a client.

The challenges were made worse for Steve by the many harmful conclusions he drew about himself as a novice in a management role. Unhelpful mental chatter such as "This is an impossible role to succeed in," "I don't know what I am doing," and "I am completely alone with this mess" was throwing him off and making it impossible to navigate the difficult path he was on. We call this type of thinking "Static" because it is like the fuzzy snow between the stations on a radio or old-fashioned television that makes you want to cover your ears and hope someone else will grab the dial and fix it.

At first, I tried to be supportive. I would encourage him to get all his concerns off his chest. Sometimes I would try to coach him gently and show him how his Static and constant negative focus on work was making his situation worse. After a few months of this however, I grew resentful. While Steve would use me as a sounding board, he wasn't trying any of the tools I offered him and I started to feel like I was his unpaid live-in coach, not his spouse.

My Static piggy-backed on his. Unhelpful thoughts such as "He cares about his work more than me and the kids," "He only pays attention when there is a problem," and "I am sick of being talked at if he won't try anything I am teaching him" only served to amplify the frustration in our home and likely reinforced some of his own Static beliefs about being alone with the mess.

What started as a handful of work problems and negative thoughts for Steve reverberated outward to set off a state of Static for him, then me, and disrupted our relationship for months.

Static thoughts are unhelpful and lead to unpleasant feelings.

If you were dealing with a major challenge, which of these two beliefs would you want to adopt?

- Belief 1: This is just too hard for me; I will never be able to figure it out.

- Belief 2: If anyone can figure it out, it's me.

I can't imagine anyone choosing the first belief on purpose. It offers nothing creative or solution-focused to apply to whatever obstacle you might be facing. Sadly, plenty of people live their lives in a state of almost perpetual Static. They feel lost, confused, and inadequate because they haven't found a tool to support them through tough mental, emotional, and spiritual states. And if you share your life with other people, the fuzzy white noise you are stuck in can impact those around you and vice versa until you are entangled in collective Static that never seems to end.

As a Superabound coach I am something of an expert on Static, having worked with it personally and professionally for years. And the good news is, I have a simple and effective tool to support you so you can recognize and move from Static to another "station"

Static thoughts are unhelpful and lead to unpleasant feelings.

of your choosing. But before you learn that tool, we first need to know the telltale signs when you are in a Static state.

How to Recognize Static

Think about your home's fire alarm for a moment. The sound is piercing, and it probably sends you into a flurry of action when it goes off. It is likely the most awful, annoying sound you will ever hear in your home.

And yet, it is intolerable by design. There is a good reason you don't see options on the market for fire alarms that sound like a gentle wind chime or that sing you a lullaby. While those would be far more pleasant, if there is smoke in the air you want a fire alarm that is going to scream at you until you deal with it and have eliminated the risk. Even if it turns out that someone just overcooked dinner, your alarm is going to treat every instance of smoke like a high-intensity emergency and respond as such.

Much like a fire alarm, you also have a high-intensity reaction to any whiff of danger. You will recognize this as an unpleasant emotion. Feelings from slight irritation to full-fledged misery are often a sign that you are between clear frequencies and somewhere in the fuzzy realm of Static.

You might read that and think, "*Wait, so you are saying that ANY time I feel even a little off I might be running into Static?*"

Yes, but don't let that overwhelm you—especially if you are someone who experiences more negative emotions than positive ones. It may not seem like it, but this is a good thing. When you feel an unpleasant emotion, it is the smoke alarm of your internal system blaring wildly to get your attention so you can assess the risk before you, put out any fires threatening your safety, and eventually make your way back to a clear and chosen frequency.

If Static didn't carry this energetic signature, you would never notice it and might go an entire lifetime operating from a set of beliefs that probably aren't helpful to you and your Vision.

Instead, Static leaves clues. And if you pay attention when it's happening, you will be able to spot it more easily, implement the process I am about to teach you, and make your way to a different station.

H.E.A.L. Static

In order to move from a Static state back into a more aligned frequency, Steve and I use four steps in an easy-to-remember format we call H.E.A.L.:

- Honor

- Experience

- Ask

- Listen

This is not a silver bullet that will rid you of every thought or emotion that slows you down, but rather a practice of attending to whatever Static state you find yourself in. Like any other tool, it is not something you will master the first time you do it, but if you commit to moving through this process regularly you will find yourself less susceptible both to landing in Static and camping out there for extended periods.

Honor

The first step may seem counterintuitive, especially since I just told you how living in Static can be so detrimental to your progress. However, to deal with Static, you can't just cover your ears, close your eyes, and hope it changes. You need your senses available to guide you. That means learning how to spot and witness your Static state long enough to troubleshoot which way to turn the dial of your attention to reach the next clear frequency.

To do this, honor your whole experience. No emotion is pesky or unwelcome. You aren't trying to fix or erase anything about yourself when you H.E.A.L. Static. The only intention with this process is to let yourself get the full guidance of your experience—intellectually, emotionally, and even spiritually. Remember, the clue that you are in Static is often an unpleasant emotion. So, when that alarm bell goes off, rather than fight or ignore the feeling, start by thanking it for being there.

You can do this out loud or in your mind. A simple "Thank you, [name the emotion], for being here and calling attention to my Static" will do perfectly.

When I noticed I was starting to feel resentful about Steve dissecting his work problems night after night, at first I told myself it was just a "rough patch." He would eventually apply for another internal role and this drama would end. But as time went on and our collective Static grew, it was like a forgotten dish on a burning stove. At first, I didn't notice the faint singed smell in the air, but the more often Steve expressed his misery and

You aren't trying to fix or erase anything about yourself when you H.E.A.L. Static.

the more my resentment grew, things started to smoke and my alarm went off.

One night as Steve was about to detail the problem of the day, I stopped him. I told him I was feeling resentful that our nightly habit had become talking about his job. Although I wanted to be supportive of him, I admitted that I felt powerless and frustrated. This was an act of honoring what I was feeling instead of stuffing it down to appear supportive. This one shift opened the door for us to have a real conversation that got us out of Static and onto a path to change the situation.

It doesn't matter if you are in a Static state alone or in collective Static with other people who share your unhelpful beliefs and feelings. Acknowledge it. Call it Static. Honor that your inner alarm system is going off and go find the smoke. And although it might feel forced at first, consider that the discomfort you are feeling right now is the best possible catalyst to move you to a better frequency. Learn to listen to your internal alarm even if it is uncomfortable. With some practice you may find that you can get through Static more quickly and peacefully by honoring its siren as soon as you can and meeting it without resistance.

Many people are practiced at intellectualizing emotions and reacting to them, but few have learned how to locate and feel emotional energy in their own bodies.

Experience

Once you have made it clear that you are coming to this exploration with respect for the Static at hand, it is time to experience both your felt sense of discomfort and the narrative surrounding it. If this is new to you, it's likely you may feel a little silly at first, or that you are just making up the answers. That is normal, but please know you can't do this wrong.

Many people are practiced at intellectualizing emotions and reacting to them, but few have learned how to locate and feel emotional energy in their own bodies. You may need a coach or supportive friend to walk you through this, but we have also created a downloadable worksheet and a meditation that you can use regularly as you get comfortable with this skill—especially if you aren't yet comfortable emoting with witnesses. You can find it at *www.beSuperabound.com/collective.*

Although I have processed thousands of emotions with clients at this point, my introduction to exploring this space came from Deep Dive Coaching founder Bev Aron. It was early on in my first coach training class and, as much as I loved the mindset tools I was learning, I was avoiding going too deep into any of the work around emotions. I thought of my emotions as big, annoying problems I wanted to solve quickly so I could get them out of the way and push on to my next goal.

Bev must have sensed me wanting to climb the walls every time there was a session on feelings because she asked if she could demonstrate some processing with me. To my surprise, the moment I went inward to sit with and notice what I thought was "just a bit of sadness" the floodgates opened, and I found myself doing what was unthinkable to me at the time: crying publicly. By the end of the session, my eyes were dry again and I felt relieved and became convinced that there was internal wisdom behind the fortress of the feelings we don't allow ourselves to feel.

Although this exercise probably won't take you as deep as you could go with a seasoned guide, this is a tool you can use to investigate

Static gently on your own any time you feel weighed down on the journey to your next Lantern.

Four Steps to Experience Your Static

Step 1: Take a breath or two and bring your attention into your body. You might do a quick scan from head to feet and notice any area that seems to need your attention. It could be in the form of tension, pressure, or the feeling of a void that shouldn't be there.

Step 2: Take your attention to that area of your body. It might help to imagine a door at this location and then step inside. Have a look around from within the experience.

Step 3: Take note of any qualities you can.
• Where is the Static located?
• Does it have a shape, a color, a pattern of movement?

Be with the experience patiently and if you can't get a read on it, you could consider:
• If this Static did have a shape or color, what would it be?
• If it did move, how might it move?
• If this were a room, how might it be decorated?

Again, don't worry if you feel like you are making up the answers. The point here is to shift your attention internally and be with your experience. It doesn't have to be detailed or especially profound. Simply give your experience your complete attention and get a felt sense of the qualities of how this Static feels for you right now.

Step 4: Notice the narrative attached to this sensation. What is the story you're telling yourself about this feeling? Don't spend too much time reinforcing the story with yourself, just get the highlights.

Ask

Once you are aware of your felt energetic experience, the next step is to ask some questions. This can be an intuitive process, or you can ask questions such as:

- What are you trying to alert me to?
- Why are you here for me right now?
- What might you be protecting me from?
- What do you want me to know?

This is not an interrogation but rather a chance for you to create an opening to spot an important insight in the middle of what might seem like fuzzy noise.

Listen

The final step in the H.E.A.L. process is to listen to what the Static is asking of you. Might this feel like you are just talking to yourself? At first, it probably will. But the act of generously considering what this internal alarm needs—to be soothed, released, managed, or heard—is powerful.

Listening is something you only do consciously when you believe that there is something worth hearing. While much of the world deals with their unhelpful feelings by trying to avoid them or find someone else to blame them on, those of us who decide to Superabound understand that Static is there for a reason.

And when you start to treat Static like there could be a nugget of wisdom there for you, you can freely ask what it needs, hear the answer, and clear the path to the next frequency you want to be on.

With your new awareness you may have a sense of how to care for yourself in the presence of this Static. It could be as simple as going for a walk, taking a nap, or writing out some ideas for next steps. You will know this to be an authentic instruction only if it feels nourishing for you. If you get back a response that is in any way harsh or self-scolding in nature, go back to the beginning because this is another layer of Static that needs to be H.E.A.L.ed.

> **While much of the world deals with their unhelpful feelings by trying to avoid them or find someone else to blame them on, those of us who decide to Superabound understand that Static is there for a reason.**

This final step of listening might be ongoing. Some of my clients have reported doing this exercise and asking their Static, "What do you need from me?" without getting a response. In those instances, I suggest you expect that the clarity will come over the next few days. Sometimes we simply need space and time to reach the next clear frequency.

In the Steve-work saga, we had an honest and open conversation where we discovered that his Static was trying to show him that he was putting unrealistic expectations on himself. He was pushing himself to succeed immediately in a brand-new role in a fast-paced, high-growth environment.

The Static for me was H.E.A.L.ed when I recognized that my internal alarm wasn't throwing a tantrum only because our conversations revolved around his miserable work life. The very first and clearest message I received from within was, "Stop coaching your husband."

The only reason Steve felt comfortable spending evenings and weekends talking about work was because I allowed it. My lack of a boundary turned our home life into a Petri dish spawning sadness and victimization in every corner. I told him that, while I loved him dearly and believed he needed a coach, it wasn't going to be me. He heard me loud and clear and began working with his own life coach the next week.

I continued to listen to what my own Static had to say. The alarm of frustration was offering me the insight that Steve's energy was focused on a workplace that didn't utilize his skills and talents as effectively as we could if we were to work together. It became clear that I was growing a business on my own and trying to be supportive of Steve when what I really wanted was more support for myself.

Through the process of listening, I heard my real desire was to have Steve as a partner not only in our marriage but also in the company I was building. This wasn't easy to bring up, but that conversation where our personal and collective Static was Honored, Experienced, Asked, and Listened to created a ripple effect that found us on the same page and resulted in growing our business together, doing what we love most.

Choose Your Obstacle

You step into the cold night, light your torch, and start walking toward the mountain before you. After a few minutes, the ground begins its gentle slope upward.

You trip on some loose rocks and start to step more cautiously, holding your torch high above your head to cast more light on the trail. After an hour you reach a fork in the path. The road to your left swings out wide and seems to dip downward. You see the dirt is tightly packed, smoothed by the feet of past travelers who went this way on the mountain toward their own lanterns.

The path to your right leads to what appears to be a dead end at a sheer rock wall. You move a little closer to get a better look and find a barely noticeable "trail" of narrow ledges jutting out of the cliff. By your estimation they are just big enough to stand on but with a backpack on and the hand holding your torch already spoken for, considering an attempt to get up that way feels dangerous.

This is your first challenge. Do you take the route on the left hoping that the path that seems to lead downward will eventually resume its climb toward your lantern?

Or do you take the direct but terrifying route upward calling upon your courage while trying to balance your torch and your backpack, which suddenly seems to have doubled in weight?

You make your decision and take your path.

Hours after crossing your chosen terrain, you find a nook that acts as a makeshift stand to rest your torch in so you can sit down and relax with both arms free. You reflect for a moment on what you learned about the mountain during this tricky part of your hike and write a note in your journal so you remember it the next time you face a similar challenge.

Once you have captured the lesson, you gaze up at the starry sky and breathe in the cool, crisp night air. You feel a sense of awe. This journey has not been easy, but making it through this first challenge has brought you closer to your lantern and you give yourself a pat on the back for getting this far.

Finally, it's time to continue your hike. You stand up, feeling stronger and more confident than before, ready to take on the next challenge on the path and every one after it until you touch your torch to your lantern and light it.

CHAPTER 8

Overcoming the Challenges

By Steve

Challenges Make You Stronger

In 2010, Ellen Daly was not yet a *New York Times* best-selling collaborative writer. At that point, early in her career, she hadn't even been to a publishing industry trade show. But as an English major and experienced editor, she was excited to attend her first: the Book Expo America, or BEA, the biggest trade show in her field.

Her Lantern was to meet prospective clients and get contracts for her ghostwriting services.

She arrived with business cards in hand, ready to make connections. But after three days, she left with an armful of free books and every single one of the business cards she had brought with her. Not only did she not get any new projects, she had gone through the entire event without speaking to anyone.

Introverts, can you relate?

Networking clearly wasn't her thing. However, she was still committed to her vision of helping high-profile people bring the book idea in their heads to life in the world. So rather than trying to force herself to strike up conversations with strangers, she found a different trail to hike.

It turned out that one of Ellen's friends was what is known as a "super-connector," who happened to have a network of the exact people Ellen wanted to work with. She asked her friend to start introducing her to folks with the content and audience to support a book but who might not have the time and expertise to write it alone.

> Challenges are the terrain—the tasks and decisions—between you and the Lantern you want to light.

As Ellen described it, "I built my business one connection at a time. Eventually I was fortunate enough to work with the founder of Aveda and things grew from there." She went on to coauthor books with John Mackey, founder and former CEO of Whole Foods, relationship expert Esther Perel, and many others. Ellen's story illustrates a simple truth about Challenges:

Challenges are the terrain—the tasks and decisions—between you and the Lantern you want to light. In Ellen's case, her Challenge was finding influential people who needed a ghostwriter and trusted her enough to hire her.

If she took the path so often recommended by "tough love" coaches and teachers, after her setback at the BEA she would have signed up for the next twenty conferences, determined to become a networking expert. She might have reached her Lantern this way, but she would have had far more Static to deal with in the process. This buildup of Static is the reason most people quit when they take the path of "try harder" with their Challenges. They're working against their existing preferences and tendencies. But she made a genius move instead and asked herself what other paths existed to cross this terrain.

Writing a book is an intimate thing, and the people Ellen wanted to work with were probably not searching for ghostwriters online or through random chance at a trade show. Rather than trying to cold call or ambush prospective clients at a conference, she took a path that would make it easier to connect with people in a low-pressure, high-trust environment.

In the end, she needed to cross the terrain between her starting place and her Lantern to meet her future clients and build trust. Enter her super-connector friend who showed Ellen that she didn't have to scale a sheer stone wall when there was a footpath just off to the side.

This is why H.E.A.L.ing Static is so important as a first step. Being in a high Static state will block you from seeing the creative ways to approach the terrain in front of you. Once you H.E.A.L. Static as a regular practice, you start to see more options for making progress toward your next Lantern.

As Ellen's story shows, there are often low-Static ways to move toward a Lantern. Not every Challenge has to feel hard.

There is no reason to burn yourself out on things that could be easy.

If you're working toward a Super-abound Vision, there will be plenty of times when the only way to make it to the next plateau is to climb the rock. But if it feels like you're scaling a boulder every day of your life, chances

There is no reason to burn yourself out on things that could be easy.

are that's the result of high Static states and not looking for other options to cross the terrain.

Yes, sometimes humans must do hard things to grow. But you won't grow faster if you stack obstacles one on top of another until you break. Finding a path forward that feels great to you is not cheating. It's simply a more sustainable, thoughtful way to light your Lantern.

Break It Down

Challenges are simple, in the end. They consist of one of two things: tasks and decisions. Anything other than a task that you can put on the calendar and complete or a decision that has a final choice is not a Challenge. It's Static.

The way to make progress on any Challenge is to break it down into its component parts. A Challenge will feel most intimidating when you look at the whole scope of what's involved, rather than seeing all the tiny tasks and relatively small decisions that comprise it. And this isn't just for big projects at work. Sometimes the Challenge in front of you is a messy kitchen.

For me, staring at my kitchen with a cityscape of half-full glasses, breakfast bowls with dried cereal inside, and semi-important papers that the kids will ask about after they're tidied up makes me want to just walk away and leave it for later. Dealing with the mess right now feels overwhelming. But the moment I commit and put just one dish where it goes, I feel like I've cracked the code.

There is no project that cannot be broken down into simpler, more doable chunks.

It may be a small Challenge but the path to a clean kitchen starts by handling just a single dish and repeating the process until it's all done.

There is no project that cannot be broken down into simpler, more doable chunks. And there are countless ways to do this. Let's say you want to create a new product offering for your business. Having a conversation with a colleague is one way to start breaking it down. Where before you only had an idea in your mind, now you have another person who shares that idea and can flesh it out with you. Creating a document is another way to break it down. You now have the idea residing with two people and your first artifact: a plan. That plan—even if it's as rudimentary as an intentional sentence about the Lantern you want to light and some possibilities for getting there— can be shared to more people to put the idea into their minds.

Taking the plan and entering the first few tasks and decisions into a spreadsheet or calendar is another step on the path up your mountain. With a list of things to do and dedicated time to do them, you turn something as monumental as creating a brand-new product into something doable that you and your team can work on each day.

The steps for making sustainable progress on any Challenge can be remembered by the 5Rs, which are:

- *Resolve*: Decide what's next and H.E.A.L. any Static you find yourself in.

- *Respond*: Do what's next, H.E.A.L. Static as needed.

- *Reflect*: What tools will you keep as you climb up the mountain toward this next Lantern and what will you leave behind?

- *Rest*: Take real care of yourself and do what you need to be ready to move forward.

- *Repeat*: Keep going until your Lantern is lit.

A client of ours, Mike Caronna, is a media executive and inventor of the 3D Stick. It's a tool that lets journalists and storytellers capture 3D images without spending a quarter of a million dollars on a high-tech rig that doesn't travel well. As a journalist and VR fan, Mike saw a gap in the market for something portable and inexpensive that still creates high-quality 3D images. He wanted to build something that would enable people to tell immersive stories even without a massive budget.

Between his idea and first 3D Stick sold, Mike had a series of Challenges to move through. One of them was to launch the website so people could buy the product. Here's how we worked through the 5Rs to help him get there.

- *Challenge:* Launch the website
- *The Lantern this Challenge helps him get closer to*: Selling the first 3D Stick

Starting with *Resolve*, there were a few decisions Mike had to make. These included:

- *Where to host his website?*
- *What domain should he use?*
- *How much should he charge?*
- *What was the best way to show his product?*

You may look at this list and think, "No big deal." And that is the beauty of Challenges: On paper, they tend not to be all that exciting. It's when we get in our own way that these decisions become much harder to act on.

In Mike's case, he was a first-time inventor, and each of these steps meant entering an unknown future where his work would be on display for everyone to see, and potentially judge. As you can imagine, this brought up plenty of Static for him. So with each decision, he also made room for the voices within that told him not to go through with it. H.E.A.L.ing Static was the path around Mike's fear of people not understanding his idea. Instead of letting that fear stop him, he was able to get to work on what really mattered.

Once the first decisions were made and the path was clear, it was time for Mike to *Respond* and get to work. His tasks included mostly mundane things like signing up with an e-commerce provider, creating a sales page for the 3D Stick, and setting the price.

The Respond phase is often a list of tasks and to-dos between you and your next milestone. When Mike went to build the sales page, he was excited at first and finished it in a single day. But when a week had passed and he hadn't shared it with anyone yet, I asked what Static may be in his way. It turned out the fear of being judged was again preventing him from taking the next step. Bringing awareness to this allowed him to regain his momentum and get his social media game underway.

The Respond phase looks like action. Sometimes lots of it. This is when you put your head down, silence all the distractions, and do the tasks that will move you a step closer to your Lantern.

What many people find is that simply beginning the Respond phase opens up new possibilities for them. By doing this kind of focused, deliberate activity—where your decisions are made and your purpose is clear—a source of energy, creativity, and even joy can emerge. It's the opposite of procrastinating or doubting yourself. It's losing yourself in the work because you know what's to be done next and why it matters.

With Mike's website out in the world, you might think that the first Challenge toward his Lantern was complete. However, there were two more phases before crossing this task off the list: *Reflect* and *Rest*.

Most people skip the Reflect phase, but Superabounding means growing and learning to become wiser for the future. Rather than doing what's easiest and just plugging along, the next step is to Reflect. Without this deliberate pause, you may miss out on the insight from your experiences. On your hike up the mountain to your Vision, the Reflect stage is the equivalent of periodically making sure you have the correct gear at hand. It's clearing mud off your hiking boots and refueling your torch so you'll be ready for the next patch of terrain, rather than pressing on thinking you'll move faster if you just keep going.

After his site was live, Mike took some time to Reflect. He looked at his work and made a list of areas to improve and things he learned about the software he was using.

For many Challenges, the Reflect step could look like gathering and analyzing data. Mike might feel good about launching the site, but does it get him closer to making sales? Reflecting is where you see the Challenge in the context of the Lantern you are trying to light and start to think about what the next Challenge might be.

Another critical piece of the Reflect phase is to celebrate the small victories. When you celebrate your achievements, you notice how you've grown and can appreciate the capacities within you. This builds the confidence that you can keep going.

So many people think that celebrations are reserved for the end of the line only, when the Lantern is lit. But celebrating your progress is an act of self-worth. It says that you are worthy of acknowledgment and that your efforts matter.

Celebrating your progress is an act of self-worth.

Encouragement also tends to be a hard one for many people to offer themselves. It's tough to break the habit of chasing goals in order to prove yourself or to show someone that they were wrong for doubting you. The idea that we can and should offer ourselves words of warmth and encouragement can fly in the face of what our culture sees as strength and "mental toughness."

But when you give yourself encouragement and warmth, you ensure that no one else has to be your cheerleader for you to make progress. You become more resilient and less prone to burnout since you aren't waiting for others to appreciate your work. You're doing it for yourself.

This brings us to *Rest*, which is the part most people forget about entirely. After all, it looks the most like "being lazy." We've been trained to think that if we're not actively rushing toward the next Lantern, we're wasting time. And while it's true that rest sometimes looks like doing a lot of nothing, what's happening on the inside is important.

The body, mind, and even the spirit need rest to become stronger. It's why elite athletes invest just as much into their recovery protocols as they do into their training. Remember my bike ride up Haleakalā, the 10,000-foot volcano on Maui? It was my regular rest stops that gave my legs and mind the strength to make it all the way to the top.

In a world that praises hustle you might have adopted collective Static thoughts such as "I can sleep when I'm dead" or "Working harder is the only way to succeed." But the latest research shows, the less sleep you get, the closer you probably are to bringing about your own final day.

Rest, far from being demotivating or slowing your progress, is energizing. When you take a real pause from your work, you fill up your inner source of power. No matter how inspiring your Vision is, there are some days you just need to get lost in a good book or prioritize having fun with your family and friends to let yourself enjoy the vista from the part of the mountain you just climbed. After all, you're not a Lantern-lighting robot. When you bake Rest into your plan, you ensure you have ample energy for the next leg of the journey.

Practicing the 5Rs together helps you break down the tangle of terrain between you and your next Lantern into doable steps with plenty of space to take care of yourself along the way. In Mike's case, he rested by publishing the homepage for the 3D Stick once it was good—not perfect—and closing the lid of his computer when his kids came home from school. He spent the rest of the day with his family, which, if you've ever worked on a website project, you know what an accomplishment it is not to obsess endlessly over it until every pixel is perfect.

> **When you bake Rest into your plan, you ensure you have ample energy for the next leg of the journey.**

Finally, reenergized and ready to keep moving, you *Repeat*. Challenges are not complete until your Lantern is actually lit. So if there is still terrain to be crossed until you can touch your torch to the wick and see the flame before you, then you must Repeat the 5Rs.

But when you Repeat the 5Rs, you aren't just doing the same thing over and over. You may be starting from the beginning of the process, but you're at a new point now. This is because you've made progress from overcoming earlier Challenges! You now have new decisions to make (Resolve), new actions to take based on them (Respond), new lessons to learn from those actions (Reflect), and a new position at which to recharge (Rest).

Challenges Show Commitment

The five Rs are the key to crossing the terrain from where you are now to where your Lantern is waiting to be lit. But the Superabound mindset shift toward these sometimes tedious or unwelcome Challenges is to see them as a chance to recommit to your Vision. This turns them from being problems in your life to clarifying moments on your journey.

When you're engaged with a task that requires your strength and your will, any doubts you may be harboring about your Vision or your next Lantern will be revealed. Without the Challenge before you, those doubts—which are forms of Static—will likely just be hanging out in the background of your mind. After all, there's not much of a reason for them to surface if you're not disrupting the status quo yet.

But the moment you take on the next Challenge, the voices of doubt get triggered and suddenly come to the surface. In this way, Static behaves like a non-Newtonian fluid such as corn starch dissolved in water (or "oobleck" for the Dr. Seuss fans out there). It flows when poured and will run through your fingers when you try to hold it, but as soon as you press on it, it becomes a solid. What seems like a liquid, providing no real impediment to your journey, becomes like a brick wall as soon as you provide the pressure of a Challenge. That change in state could look like procrastination, complaining, strategic forgetfulness, and ultimately backing down from a Challenge you're engaged in.

This phenomenon became clear to me in a big way as I worked through Challenges toward a recent Lantern. While my first career was playing trumpet, the first instrument I actually learned was piano. I played all the way through high school and even a year of music school afterward, but I never reached anything near virtuoso level.

And I hadn't played for twenty years when I finally decided to get a piano for our home.

I brought my standard intensity to the project of relearning piano and wanted to explore my outer limits. As such, I wasn't satisfied just with ambient improvisations or rehashing songs from my high school studies. As I was daydreaming about what would be the most epic thing I could do on piano, at some point in my life, *way* off in the distant future, I saw myself playing a moving performance of Beethoven's fifth piano concerto, in full, by memory, for an audience. I had first fallen in love with this piece, called the "Emperor Concerto," while playing the trumpet part in the orchestra, and I thought that if I could ever sit down and play it on piano that would be a real milestone moment in my life.

So, with not a small amount of trepidation and doubt, I started working with a teacher. In a testament to the power of having a coach, her faith in me that I could play all 1,000+ bars of this monumental piece was a core reason I was able to keep going through all the Challenges. And yet, the scale of the Challenges tested my commitment to lighting this particular Lantern. Many times.

Throughout the two years I spent learning the piece, I would turn a new page, after having worked on the previous pages for weeks, and find myself thinking, "It's no use. There are just too many notes, moving too fast. This section will be too hard." Similar resistance came up when it came time to schedule a performance, "It's not good enough to play for people yet. I can't figure out the logistics of putting on a performance."

None of those excuses would have arisen if I didn't have the Lantern of actually performing the whole piece for a live audience. If I was just doing it as my schedule, life, and piano skills permitted, I wouldn't have had to stretch. And I definitely wouldn't have done anything remotely scary or nerve-wracking, like putting on a performance of it in front of people I didn't know. Each of those Challenges brought me to a deeper place of commitment, precisely because something was at stake to overcome them. Learning the next page meant time, patience, and brain power were at stake. Scheduling a performance meant I could no longer have "someday" as the comfortable non-date in my mind, but would soon be faced with the real and raw "now" as the performance time.

Each Challenge along the path toward that performance day and beyond served as an opportunity to remind myself why I was doing it in the first place, and why my Lantern mattered. Anything from the simple and present, "I love making music," to the more zoomed out and future-oriented, "I'm doing this to grow and share something beautiful with people," would serve as my recommitment during Challenges.

> **The fact is, there's only so much we can learn about ourselves or our commitment through journaling or self-reflection alone.**

And when the time came to perform the piece in public, I did so for one of our clients, as part of a company-wide workshop on lighting Lanterns. The ability to share this incredible work of art together with ideas on how to make progress on important things in work and life made lighting my Lantern that much more meaningful toward my Vision.

The fact is, there's only so much we can learn about ourselves or our commitment through journaling or self-reflection alone. These tools are wonderful, but if we wait until we feel 100 percent confident about something or until all the Static is gone, we will never take on the big tasks that lead to real progress and ultimately change us. The mountain itself and the struggle it offers help us to discover who we are.

Take, for example, a committed relationship with a life partner. How would you know how much you loved them if every day were easy street? Imagine they never got sick, never bugged you in any way, always had perfect hair, and never required anything of your time or energy to connect with them. It would be hard to know if you really cared for your partner in a meaningful way or if it was just convenient and easy.

Erin and I often joke that couples should have to start their relationship in two different countries, like we did. If you're willing to go through years of video calls, cross-border travel logistics, and residency applications just to be together, that says something about your relationship. Every time we got on a plane, drove for hours, rearranged our lives to see each other or packed up and moved to another country (which we've both done), it was a step up the mountain toward the life we wanted to create together. Those acts of commitment showed both of us how much we valued our shared Vision.

The Superabound Challenge Mindset

The key to Superabounding with Challenges lies in shifting your mindset toward them from something to be avoided to something to be embraced. When you believe that the terrain before you is not only the path to your next Lantern but will even *help* you grow in ways that matter to your future, then your interest in taking them on will soar.

Many people's near-instant response to Challenges is, "Why is this happening to me?" But that question robs you of your agency and power in

> The far more empowering question for a Challenge is, "Why is this here *for* me?"

the situation. It casts you as a victim, the unfortunate target of a cruel world. Most importantly, it shuts down the part of the brain responsible for creativity, thoughtfulness, and communication. The far more empowering question for a Challenge is, "Why is this here *for* me?"

That question makes you a partner with the world, including any difficult situations. You have a role in everything that happens to you, even if that role is simply being who you are in that place at that time. If you believe as we do that the Universe is a collaborator in your life, and even has a dream for you in some way, then whatever obstacle you're facing in this moment must be part of that dream. Chances are the reason is not so you can give up.

For example, when Erin and I encounter a thorny issue in our business, we do our best to make space for it. We go for walks to get our bodies moving and thoughts flowing. We brainstorm ideas for how the issue fits within the life the Universe is dreaming for us. We look for what she calls the "$10,000 lessons" it holds for our company. And at the end of the process, which sometimes takes days or even weeks, we're more aligned with our Vision and more excited for our path forward than we were before.

> **When you see hardship as a puzzle you get to solve, or as a training partner that can help you grow and deepen your Vision, you tap into your true essence.**

When you see hardship as a puzzle you get to solve, or as a training partner that can help you grow and deepen your Vision, you tap into your true essence. The emotional stamp of that essence is joy.

Finding joy in Challenges is what it means to Superabound on the path to your next Lantern.

Don't Let the Fire Burn Out

It's been hours since you last set down your torch and breathed in the night air. This most recent leg of the journey has been incredibly hard, but you know the lantern is ahead and your determination to light it spurs you on. Your feet ache with every step over the sharp rocks and your throat is burning for water. You ignore the cries of your body and move faster in spite of them.

You are out beyond the shelter of the trees now. This terrain is intense and the wind whips around as you strain to take step after step. Suddenly the path before you goes dark. You look frantically at your torch, its fire almost completely snuffed out by the wind.

You crouch down low beside it, shielding the fire from the wind with your body. The flame spits sadly and you know that in your push to reach the lantern you have neglected the very thing you will need to light it with: the torch that holds your fire.

You stay low for a few minutes, willing the flame to stabilize, and give yourself a chance to rest.

As the fire regains strength you say a silent "thank you," promising yourself that you won't get so focused on reaching the lantern that you forget to tend your flame. Because if that flame goes out, even if you are next to the lantern you wanted to light, you will be stuck alone on the mountain in the dark.

CHAPTER 9

Tending Your Flame

By Erin

Self-Invest with the Tending Triad

We've all done it. With a powerful Vision in mind and the next Lantern closer with each Challenge overcome, we yearn to race toward that next milestone—promising ourselves we will rest when we arrive.

Equipped with the Progress Formula, you now have the practical tools to deal with the terrain along the route (your Challenges) and ways to handle the roller coaster of beliefs and emotions that will inevitably come up (Static). But there are a few more essentials that will make the journey to your next Lantern one you can complete with energy to spare.

At the beginning of this book, I told you all about the year I burned out, shut down two businesses, and almost ended my engagement with Steve—which would have meant a life without him, our children, and the many adventures we have had. My own inner fire got very low and nearly went out because I didn't know how to tend to it.

And while I hope you gain countless tools and insights from this book, the most important one of all is what we call the "Tending Triad."

The Tending Triad is not just a tool for you to use once in a while. It is a line in the sand that separates those who Superabound from those who just run after their goals, ignoring their well-being as they go. Because of the experience I have had, I feel strongly that the Tending Triad is nonnegotiable when it comes long-term wellness and sustainable success.

Many people talk about self-care, but they don't go far enough to actually integrate those practices into their lifestyle. To make progress toward your Vision month after month, year after year, you need to go further than just caring for yourself when you have time, and actually *self-invest.*

It's easy to take a nap or a few days off and check self-care off your list for the month as you run screaming back to attack your latest goal in the swamp. But like long-term financial investing, the Tending Triad compounds over time until your personal self-investments pay dividends.

The Tending Triad consists of three practices that are used together to keep your inner fire burning bright through the process of making progress toward your Vision. Your "inner fire" is a way to think about your energy, inspiration, and drive. Like actual fire, it needs heat (your passion), fuel (resources that sustain you such as sleep, nourishment, and community), and oxygen (room to step back and breathe). Unfortunately, some people don't consider the state of their inner fire until it is on the brink of fizzling out.

It's no wonder why the phenomenon is known to many as burnout. Anyone who has experienced it knows all too well how deeply they wish they could go back in time and stop their former selves from cutting corners on sleep, food, movement, and relationships. They might wish they had stuck with that yoga class or meditation practice. They lament not hiring that coach or mentor to help them set better boundaries between work and downtime.

The deep dark times come after burning out. There may be days where you can barely muster the energy to get out of bed in the morning. And if you somehow manage to keep crawling along the path to your next Lantern, lighting it holds little joy or significance for your larger Vision.

> **The Tending Triad is a lifestyle that, when embraced, not only helps you stay focused on the things that matter, but will prevent you from taking a long and painful detour because your inner fire was so dim you couldn't see where you were heading.**

The Tending Triad is a lifestyle that, when embraced, not only helps you stay focused on the things that matter, but will prevent you from taking a long and painful detour because your inner fire was so dim you couldn't see where you were heading.

I began self-investing during one of the lowest points in my life, and Steve and I spent years experimenting with ourselves before teaching it. After recognizing I had to make a major life change, I shut down my businesses and moved to Boston for the summer with Steve. I was in a country I didn't have a work visa for and therefore couldn't busy myself with a job. Although I didn't know it at the time, it was in fact the perfect situation for me to establish a Tending Triad and learn how to care for my own inner flame.

Fuel, Heat, and Oxygen

To have a long-lasting, strong fire, you need fuel.

When I landed in Boston, burnt out and in constant pain, I had terrible personal wellness habits. I slept only six hours a night on average due to years of going to bed late and waking up early to teach yoga. My eating schedule was all over the place as I had trained myself to delay meals to accommodate classes and clients. And my own physical exercise was sporadic as I fit it in only when convenient or on the rare days I had little pain.

Finally understanding the toll this way of living had taken on me, I began to implement true fuel for myself in the form of Sustaining Rituals. For me this looked like sleeping eight to nine hours a night and napping whenever I felt tired, no questions asked. I ate when I was hungry, walked at least twenty minutes a day around the pier where we lived, and joined a local fitness studio to start taking classes.

As my body started to respond to this fuel I was feeding it, I discovered the next ingredient to a strong inner fire. While I was learning how to finally take great care of myself, Steve was working full time. I watched my soon-to-be husband day after day exhibit something that seemed strange (and something annoying given the chronic pain I was in). He seemed to be having fun in nearly everything he did. He was authentically passionate about his life and his work. Witnessing Steve's way of being and his near constant vitality showed me the next key piece of the triad: heat.

Steve was living his life with passion pouring out of him and as I watched, I started to wonder what truly fired me up. And like many people who let their inner flame dwindle, it took a lot of trial and error to find a project I felt passionate about. After a few months I decided on a Lantern I had wanted to light since I was a child but never made the time for: to write my first book. This was the birth of the Visionary Practice, which we will teach you shortly. It is a powerful way to keep your inner fire bright and strong as you do bold things.

The final component of the Tending Triad is one that no fire can live without: oxygen. And for your inner fire, oxygen represents the Personal Filter. It is the protected space you have around yourself to breathe, literally and metaphorically. As I slowly started to regain mobility and recover from my illness, I noticed something interesting. If I spent time with people who complained constantly, I felt more drained and physically sore for days afterward. But on the days I was alone or with people who had more positive mindsets, I felt good.

At the time, Personal Filter was not something I considered to be a core component of my healing, so I had a paper-thin energetic barrier between me and the people around me. I remember on one occasion silently sitting through an entire meal while the people I was with trash talked someone they both knew. Instead of telling the group I was uncomfortable with the conversation or leaving, I sat there awkwardly just hoping the bill would arrive.

The Personal Filter is, for most people, the hardest thing to put into place and maintain. The reason is that it often requires you to have uncomfortable conversations with other people out of respect for your own well-being. We will go into more detail about how to start working with your Personal Filter later in this section of the book, but for now, know that the point of this "oxygen" is to make room for you to flourish without allowing unnecessary external Static to distract or disempower you. This practice may be the most challenging, but I assure you the payoff to your own energy and focus is worth it.

FUEL - Sustaining Rituals

Visionary Practice

By Steve

When Erin first started her coaching business, she was looking after our two-year-old daughter, Audrey, and newborn son, Julian, during the day while I was at work. For anyone who has ever looked after two children under age three, you know that there's not much room for deep thought, much less for working on a business during that time. It's play, clean, sing, make food, feed, clean again, go outside, cajole, repeat until bedtime.

So, she created a practice we've both used ever since, called Solo Soul Time. When I was looking after Audrey and Julian in the morning, when most parents feel they "must" be with their children, Erin would close the door to another room in the house and leave behind the role of "Mama."

Alone with her thoughts, she journaled about the coaching business she wanted to build. She tended to the dream in her heart of a magical, lucrative company, tuning out the crying in the background and connecting with a version of herself in the future that already had the business that present-day Erin wanted. She would ask her future self how she built her brand and coached inspiring clients.

Those sessions of visionary, inward reflection gave her ideas and confidence for growing her business. So when she had pockets to work on it, the fire was burning bright within her, and she wasted no time. Not only did she start making money, but the company went from zero to $12,000 its first year, $57,000 the next year, and $226,000 after that. She also wrote her next two books and published over 150 podcast episodes during that short time.

What enabled her to make such remarkable progress while simultaneously being the primary caregiver for two little ones was the uniquely potent combination of inner reflection and outer action. Like an in-breath and an out-breath, connecting with your Vision and putting in the work go together to make your Visionary Practice, which is the "heat" component of the Tending Triad.

Visionary Practice uses the power of your mind to create belief in your desired future.

Visionary Practice uses the power of your mind to create belief in your desired future. This matters because when you first say you want something, it's more of a wish than a belief. If the Lantern you want to light is inspiring enough, it will be beyond your current capacity to light. And most people don't factor in their ability to grow when considering what's possible in their lives.

To transform your desire from a wish (something you hope will happen) into a belief (something you *know* will happen) you need more than just action. You need to see, taste, touch, hear, and feel your Lantern being lit. This inner connection to your ideal future will give your daily work a powerful boost of magic. This is because you won't be burdened by self-doubt. The Vision in your heart is your secret treasure, giving your actions a different level of energy and purpose.

A Visionary Practice helps you step outside the status quo of your life as it has been and evolve in the ways that your Lantern requires. This works because the status quo is what has created your life so far. Seeing in a new way enables you to operate in a new way, which is what brings you closer to your next Lantern.

In Erin's case, embracing Solo Soul Time meant dropping the belief that having young children meant she couldn't be a successful entrepreneur, or that she needed to spend the mornings with the kids to be a "good" mother.

Doing this daily practice allowed her to connect with the future that she wanted, tune her mind to it, and do the work to make it a reality. The Tending Triad is a lifestyle, and it is ever evolving. Erin had a commitment not to burn out again but kids often have other plans. She had to evolve her Triad to meet the new reality of parenthood and the demands it placed on her body, mind, and spirit.

Belief Doesn't Happen in Your Head

The most common mistake people make when doing any kind of inner work (such as meeting with their future self, affirmations, and visualizations) is spending time inwardly then doing nothing. Fantasizing about a potential future may feel good, but if you aren't responding to your inner wisdom with action in the world, you aren't doing Visionary Practice.

Visionary Practice is the tangible expression of your inner belief.

When you clearly and truly want to light your next Lantern, your life will look different. You rearrange priorities, spending time and energy on things that move you toward your destination. This shift toward action, ignited by your belief in your Lantern being lit, is how you free yourself from being a victim of your life and start becoming the author instead.

If there are more excuses in your head than actions logged toward your dream, you haven't yet found your Visionary Practice. Like a job seeker giving up on the process after a handful of rejections and unanswered emails, you let the flame fizzle based on what others are doing and thinking.

Visionary Practice makes lighting your next Lantern all but inevitable, because it's your source of enduring passion for the process itself. It helps you show up day after day, gaining feedback and experience to hone your offering to the world into something extraordinary.

Want to run a marathon? You need to have a habit of logging miles to create a base layer of endurance and strength. Then, you need to sign up for an actual race, as evidence of your belief that you can do it.

Want a great relationship? You need to put in the effort to have meaningful connections with your partner that will lead to trust and intimacy over time. To make it visionary, you can also write in a journal about why your relationship matters to you.

Want to create the next $100 billion company? You need a process for building your product, creating customers, gathering feedback, and tweaking the system—all fueled by your Vision for why you're doing the work. The Visionary Practice that

> **Visionary Practice is the tangible expression of your inner belief.**

you build for yourself and your team will make you more resilient in the face of setbacks and poised for growth as you learn.

The process is not glamorous. It is work and dedication to the next Lantern and the Vision it illuminates. But it's also effective and rewarding. Visionary Practice builds confidence through increasing your skill, experience, and belief all at the same time.

Purpose, No Matter the Pressure

Some people don't find their Visionary Practice until the chips are down and the stakes are high. Nick Pope was one of them. He had no shortage of people around him saying that he would never amount to anything, and that he would be a deadbeat dad.

He first became a dad midway through high school, while his sights were set on being a professional hockey player. A driven athlete who had no qualms about sacrificing teeth for the sake of winning games, he spent the first few years of his daughter's life on the road training and playing with an NHL farm team, spending little time with his new family.

Eventually he reached a decision point and gained clarity on his Vision. It wasn't hockey itself that mattered to him, but giving his best for those who counted on him and helping his people win. It used to be his teammates on the ice—hence the captain or alternate captain letters on every jersey he'd ever played in. But he decided it was time to switch paths up the mountain from team hockey to team family. He chose real estate, setting his sights on becoming a real estate entrepreneur. He funded the journey through work in a factory, pulling sixteen-hour shifts at times. But he held true to his Vision despite the long hours and pursued his real estate license during off-hours.

He was making progress toward his intention to leave the factory and become a realtor, but he wasn't there yet. Then one day, Nick's parents announced that their Christmas gift to his family was tickets to Disney World. His now six-year-old daughter was elated. Nick said a curse under his breath and broke into a cold sweat.

It's not that he didn't love Disney. He just didn't have the money to finance the rest of the trip. And there was no way he would tell his daughter that she wasn't going to see Mickey Mouse. So, he and his wife took turns visiting a fast-cash high-interest loan shop and took out over $10,000 to fund their vacation. When it was all over, Nick found himself deeper in debt than he'd been before, with no plan for how to pay it back.

Nick's Lantern snapped into focus: he was going to launch his real estate business not only to pay back the loans before creditors came knocking but to get out of the cycle of shift work at the factory so he could enjoy more time with his family. He knew what he wanted to do and why he wanted to do it.

He was fueled by a belief in himself that was stronger than the doubt of the people around him who thought he would never escape his life choices. He eventually passed his real estate exam, was certified, and started selling houses in the area. One day at a time, and one relationship at a time, Nick stood out as a business owner who was all in, just like he had been on the hockey rink.

He was determined to know more about his home listings and be more responsive on the phone than anyone else. His Visionary Practice was to study his listings and answer the phone any time it rang. Combining that work in the world with his inner belief that he could create a thriving company, his business grew.

Now he has a team of agents that sell with him and he paid off his Disney loan long ago. Even though his path forward was sparked by a series of predicaments, first being a teenage dad then getting deep into debt, Nick stayed connected to the Vision he discovered at his hockey crossroads, and never let go.

It's easy to read Nick's story and think that it was the pressure of the loan that forced him to get serious about his Lantern. Many people have similar stories, where a catalyzing event is what they believe nudged them toward a big life change. But a more empowering way to see situations like this is that the pressure gives clarity on what matters most. These are moments when we choose our own future as we want it to be, rather than waiting for things to unfold according to someone else's plan.

Making a choice that adds pressure to your situation is certainly not necessary for growth, but it can be a catalyst for clarity and for aligning your priorities behind a Visionary Practice.

Now, while the name might sound transcendent, it's important to note that Visionary Practice is not always pleasant. In fact, the experience of doing it tends to be about 80 percent boring, 10 percent painful, 9 percent interesting, and maybe 1 percent fulfilling. This is the truth of Visionary Practice: The activities that make all the difference in your growth toward your Lantern tend not to feel exciting. Ask any athlete training for a big event. Most of what they're doing is building their baseline fitness and preparing their bodies and minds for the work ahead.

This is because an effective Visionary Practice is one in which you move, change, and grow. And moving away from what you've known is often uncomfortable and doesn't have a shortcut. Even during exciting times of growth, such as a start-up doubling in size over six months, it's still a day-by-day grind of hiring, onboarding, training, aligning. The results are exciting, but the process is a true discipline.

Your Visionary Practice is the daily activity to align your life and mind with your Lantern. As such, in those moments when Visionary Practice does feel particularly good, it is usually because you are acting from a place of integrity. You are putting time and energy toward the Vision you hold most dear. But the daily experience of growth toward the future is often hard.

You are retuning your system to be in alignment with your Lantern. Again, if you were already attuned to it, you'd be there. The practice is a way to reshape your life and train yourself to think differently.

It's how you turn your physical, mental, emotional, and spiritual being into one that is capable of lighting your Lantern. The milestone itself may never actually come to pass, but if you put in the work to become the person who *could* achieve it, then you are in the best possible position to do so.

> **Your Visionary Practice is the daily activity to align your life and mind with your Lantern.**

Sustaining Rituals

Humans are not work machines. We need to maintain healthy bodies, minds, and spirits if we want to have our greatest possible impact. As such, your Visionary Practice—where you take consistent steps toward your Lantern, both in the outside world and in your inner world of belief—must be surrounded by Sustaining Rituals. These are the things you do on a regular basis that provide fuel for the heat of your Visionary Practice to burn.

Sustaining Rituals are the habits you form to ensure that the person you are when you light your next Lantern is well in all ways. They are how you care for your precious life in the here and now while pursuing a future that matters. Sustaining Rituals are self-investment at the purest level and don't have to be creative or sexy. They don't have to cost much in terms of time, money, or energy either. Drinking a glass of water can be part of your larger ritual of creating vibrant physical health.

Sustaining Rituals are a critical part of the Tending Triad because the most important part of lighting a Lantern is not the result, but the process of getting there. After all, you will spend 99 percent of your time in the process and only a few moments actually lighting your next Lantern. And if the process of getting there saps you of energy, health, and joy, it is not worth it and isn't sustainable in pursuit of your larger Vision.

> **Sustaining Rituals are a critical part of the Tending Triad because the most important part of lighting a Lantern is not the result, but the process of getting there.**

Crafting Sustaining Rituals that serve you is how you set yourself up for long-term progress that doesn't sacrifice the most important parts of your life. Their purpose is to support your internal landscape—your physical, mental, emotional, and spiritual well-being. When you take stock of those aspects of your life and you feel that everything is covered, then your Sustaining Rituals are in good order.

The reason they are so important is not just because we want the journey to be as rewarding as the destination, but because without Sustaining Rituals in place we may not even complete the journey.

The stories of physical burnout, relationship implosion, or mental and spiritual turmoil ruining someone's progress toward their Lantern are actually more common than all the success stories we hear. We just don't hear about all the troubles because most people prefer to hide their setbacks and only talk about the high points.

How to Choose Your Rituals

An effective Sustaining Ritual gives you more energy than it requires. For instance, physical exercise requires energy but, when done at an appropriate level and with ample recovery time, gives you much more in return. Your levels of vitality, joy, and fulfillment all grow from having the right Sustaining Rituals in your life.

When selecting yours, it's likely that you have anywhere from three to ten Sustaining Rituals already present in your life. Anything that tends to your well-being in a way that compounds over time will work.

With the options wide open, what do you choose right now and why? There is no wrong answer, so you can play with this and even let it be part of your intuitive development. What brings you joy and would add value and richness to your life?

Once you choose the Sustaining Rituals you want to cultivate, try putting one on your calendar every day for mind, body, spirit, and relationships. If you are doing one thing every day with the intention to support those facets of your life, and you do that consistently for even a single week, you will notice a change in your well-being.

Committing to your Sustaining Rituals by scheduling them and showing up regularly is how you invest in yourself for the long term. They become your insurance policy against burnout by giving you all the life energy, or fuel for the fire, to make the climb toward your Vision.

Personal Filter

When you've committed to your Visionary Practice and are investing in Sustaining Rituals, the final piece of the Tending Triad is having room to breathe—a Personal Filter.

Your Personal Filter allows you to have the time and space that support you best. It is oxygen for your inner flame.

A Superabound life can be more intense than the norm. That's because following your Vision requires having a sense of purpose and meaning that most people haven't considered and may not even believe is possible.

To live at this new level, you need space.

Consider what happens to your energy when you're surrounded by people who have a more negative outlook. It's not fun. Notice what drains your vitality and dampens the spark of your inner flame. It could be overconsumption of the news or of social media. It might even be a well-meaning relative with a habit of dropping in unannounced to share their latest tales of woe.

Your Personal Filter allows you to have the time and space that support you best. It is oxygen for your inner flame.

Everything that just came to mind for you is what you can address with your Personal Filter. You want a barrier in place to protect your energy and not let the Static of the outside world diminish your flame or overpower your Vision.

As human beings—especially if we're stretching our limits on the path to our next Lantern—we already have plenty of Static to deal with. Is it really necessary to read your cousin's social media rants or to watch the horrific news of the day at 11:00 p.m. before trying to go to sleep?

Rather than allowing into your space anything or anyone that wants to reach you and wondering why you feel depleted, start reinforcing your Personal Filter. It may not seem like it at first, but this protected space you give yourself is an act of commitment toward your next Lantern. It will breathe even more life into you that you can use for both your Sustaining Rituals and Visionary Practice.

In other words, it's a turbo boost for your progress up the mountain.

Signs the Filter Has Holes

You know you don't have a strong Personal Filter when you consistently resent other people. Resentment is a sign that you're doing things you don't want to do to appease others or to make them like you. It's the opposite of living from your Vision.

Another sign of a weakened Personal Filter is when you feel overstretched from being pulled in many directions. You have trouble saying no to things that aren't aligned for you. And if you do manage to say no to people, you are so consumed with guilt and fear you may be judged that you can't even enjoy the space you created.

When you are willing to suffer to try to make others comfortable, you are not tending your inner flame.

When you are willing to suffer to try to make others comfortable, you are not tending your inner flame.

It's not just other people and their energy that your Personal Filter protects you from. Your sources of information and entertainment affect your vitality as well.

Many people tell themselves they don't have time for a Visionary Practice or Sustaining Rituals, and yet somehow are able to check all their news feeds, social feeds, email inboxes, and text messages every hour. If that's true for you, a Personal Filter will be a game changer as you make space for what matters by letting go of what doesn't.

On an even more subtle level, your Personal Filter is also about how you talk to yourself and what ideas you choose to believe. Many people struggle to make the progress they want in life because they believe the voices in their heads that say they're not good enough.

One of my mentors made the biggest leaps in her business, going from several hundred thousand dollars in revenue per year to many millions in revenue, when she decided she would no longer listen to her voices of self-doubt and criticism.

Yes, you can filter your own shit-talking voices within.

The Power of a Filter

When you have a strong Personal Filter, you understand that what you want and need is important. And often when you start making your own wants and needs a priority, people in your life who are used to you putting them first may get upset. For instance, if you normally RSVP "yes" to the once-a-month dinner date your old high school friends have planned, your Personal Filter may require you to pause before responding.

Rather than going out of a sense of obligation and tradition, you can put that invitation through your Personal Filter.

You might ask yourself, "*Do I enjoy these dinners? Do I feel good while I am there and afterward?*"

These simple questions will reveal a lot if you dare to ask them. If your old pals are supportive, loving, and a big part of your life, chances are you will look forward to spending time with them. On the other hand, as you reinforce your Personal Filter you might notice that in fact you RSVP "yes" and then dread those dinners month after month.

Maybe they spend every dinner rehashing the past or teasing you with the embarrassing nickname everyone used to call you when you were sixteen. As you strengthen your Personal Filter, chances are your own self-respect will outweigh the nostalgia of the dinners and you might reinvest those monthly evenings into something that is more nourishing.

> **Every extra bit of oxygen you can feed your inner fire results in a brighter flame.**

But make no mistake, the Personal Filter is the hardest part of the Tending Triad for most people. It requires you to be in the uncomfortable position of making choices that are good for you and saying no to things you used to say yes to. It means standing up for yourself and your Vision with other people.

As hard as that may be at first, establishing a strong Personal Filter has the biggest potential payoff of the Tending Triad because every extra bit of oxygen you can feed your inner fire results in a brighter flame. As you create space for your Vision to lead in your day-to-day life, you will find that it becomes a positive feedback loop. The more time and attention you give your dreams, the more ways you will see to make them come true.

The space you create with your Personal Filter will make room for bigger and richer expressions of the rituals that sustain you and the practices that move you closer to your next Lantern.

Creating Your Tending Triad

By Erin

Now that you have a deeper understanding of the elements needed to support a strong inner fire, it's time to create your own Tending Triad.

This is a personal formula, not a universal one, and you will likely find that you have some of these areas in place organically for yourself already. As you focus on each of these three parts over time, your Tending Triad will take shape and support your inner flame.

To get you started, here are some of the exercises I use regularly to bolster my own Tending Triad.

Coffee with the Oracle—Building Your Visionary Practice

I was a reluctant scheduler when I began my business. I didn't want to be hemmed in by appointments outside of my client sessions all day and rebelled against the people who told me that at some point not having a calendar would come back to bite me in the nether regions.

My calendar protest ended when I realized I was putting in a full eight hours a day in my business, even on the days my kids were out of school and going to bed most nights without a clear sense of what I had accomplished.

Out on a walk one day, I decided my next Lantern was to figure out how to double my impact and my revenue while working no more than thirty hours a week. With no clue how I would make this wild idea a reality, I made a coffee, grabbed my laptop and journal, and headed up to my favorite place to think: the meditation barn.

I sat down before the meditation altar, lit a candle, and asked the question, "How will I do this?"

Nothing happened.

I kept sitting.

Still nothing.

Then a thought occurred to me.

I was asking the question of what to do from the perspective of a person who was feeling Static in the form of confusion and over-whelmed about what to do next. Although it wasn't a bad question to ask, I was trying to decide how to proceed from the point in the journey where I knew the least—the beginning.

What if, instead, I could talk to the version of myself somewhere out there in the future who had lit the Lantern of doubling her revenue and her impact while working thirty hours a week or less?

I sank into a meditative conversation and wrote pages of notes ranging from the mindset shift I would have to embrace to a solid action plan for reducing my work hours. After that, all items went onto my calendar and were honored in my life. This regular practice of checking in with my future helped me light the Lantern of working less and more than doubling my company's impact and revenue in a very short period of time.

While there are many names for similar practices of engaging with your future self, this practice is affectionately known in our community as Coffee with the Oracle.

Coffee with the Oracle is essentially a high-level meeting with the version of yourself that has lit the Lantern you are working toward right now. This is one powerful way to establish a Visionary Practice and we have created both a meditation and walk-through for you at *beSuperabound.com/collective* to help you connect with your own

Oracle, the version of you who has already lit your next Lantern somewhere in the future.

The thing that takes this from being just a "feel-good" exercise and makes it a Visionary Practice is not the list of to-dos you give yourself. It is actually taking Vision-aligned steps regularly toward your next Lantern. Start putting these sessions on your calendar to make it easier to show up for yourself and pour energy and action into your Superabound Vision.

Deepen Your Sustaining Rituals

The good news is you probably have many Sustaining Rituals in your life already.

If you sleep seven to nine hours a night, eat nourishing foods, and take weekends off, congratulations. You're practicing some of the best Sustaining Rituals around. But if you notice you are putting your self-investment practices in the backseat during busy or stressful moments, there is room to take these rituals to the next level.

A simple way to add more solid Sustaining Rituals to your life is to make sure that on a daily or weekly basis you have time and energy set aside for something that supports you in the following areas.

Physical Nourishment

Anything you do regularly that nourishes and supports your body would be considered a Sustaining Ritual.

Are you eating foods that make you feel great or ones that drain you? How is your water intake? Are you getting enough rest? Are you doing movement and exercises that you enjoy and are appropriate for your body? These are all questions you can ask yourself to get some ideas for ways to keep your body happy.

One of my clients spends more hours in a chair than she would like. Her first Sustaining Ritual was to add in a walk to her workday. Some days she will do her meetings while on that walk and other days she simply enjoys the natural sounds around her. The point is she knows her body wants to move and walking is now a daily ritual on her calendar that she looks forward to.

Mental and Emotional Rituals

This includes anything you do regularly to support your mental and emotional energy. This could be a morning journaling practice to clear out the cobwebs clouding your thinking or a weekly session with your personal life coach.

Your ritual may be meeting with a mentor or other practitioner who is there to help you navigate the never-ending inner narrative and emotional ups and downs of life.

One of my favorite rituals in this category happens right before bed with our six-year-old. We both take out our evening journals and spend a few minutes together talking about the day. We discuss what made us proud, what made us smile, and the things that happened that we felt grateful for.

He draws a picture in his journal while I jot down a few sentences along with any insights or lessons I learned that day.

Sometimes the whole family joins in for this evening ritual and other times it is just me and my youngest, but this is by far one of the most grounding things I do mentally and emotionally to end the day and then rest.

Spiritual Sustenance

We have mentioned spiritual practice throughout this book and while I realize this is very personal and may not be part of your Tending

Triad, I do want to address it for those readers who get energy and insight from this part of life.

Spiritual rituals can be anything that makes you feel deeply connected to your inner world or your idea of the Divine. For some this is formal meditation, prayer, and ritual. For others this is spending time in nature, stargazing, or in deep philosophical conversation.

Spiritual Sustaining Rituals can also be combined with other categories of nourishment. When I was a full-time yoga teacher, many of my students came to class not only for the physical and mental workout but for an embodied spiritual experience as well. Tending your inner flame in this way is less about what you do and more about how it makes you feel.

Revitalize Your Relationship

The final area of focus for Sustaining Rituals is your relationships. When moving toward Lantern after Lantern, it is easy to get caught up in the flurry of activity and forget to nurture the important relationships in your life. My third book, *Revitalize Your Relationship*, focused solely on helping people create more loving connection with those around them. During the years I spent coaching primarily on this topic, two things became clear to me:

First, loved ones don't enjoy being afterthoughts in your life. If you treat your partner like an unpaid, live-in assistant and not like the miraculous enigma they are, you might light your next Lantern and find yourself with no one to celebrate with.

Second, relationships need tending just like every other important part of your life. One of the ways to take better care of them is to sit down with your people and plan at least one fun outing, event, or activity in the next week that everyone will look forward to. These can be as elaborate or as simple as you like. The only rule is that the time must be used for connection with the people in front of you.

If you can put your phone away and avoid any topics or activities that don't interest everyone present, you are doing this beautifully. Connect as deeply and as often as possible, and chances are you will have love along the way to your next Lantern on the mountain.

Repair Your Personal Filter

A Personal Filter is one of the subtlest and most challenging parts of the Tending Triad, because society doesn't celebrate people having healthy boundaries or creating soulful space. For most of us, creating a consistent and strong filter takes time and the support of a coach or mentor. But to get started with this process here are a few questions you can ask yourself:

- What do I love to do to create space and energy?

- What in my life leaves me drained and uninspired?

- What do I need to add to create my Personal Filter?

- What do I need to let go of to strengthen it?

The ideas that come to you will be hints about what to do next. Don't try doing everything all at once or all alone, as it could be overwhelming to suddenly go from having porous boundaries to strong ones. Instead, choose one or two ideas from the list and decide how you want to implement them in your life.

They could be as simple as stopping the social media scroll while in bed or saying no to an event that doesn't energize you. Whatever you decide to do to help you stop leaking energy, write it down and honor it. Those small steps will add up to create the space, the oxygen, you need for your inner flame to grow.

Light the Lantern

As you clamber over the large boulder in front of you, you let out an audible grunt. You feel your face relax as your feet meet the steady path once more and you take a moment to savor the smell of the surrounding tall pine trees lining either side of the path. The trees look like giants in the dark and they sway in a way that feels comforting and protective to you and the flame you carry.

That's when you see it. At the end of the procession of trees is a rocky outcropping and on it, set deep in the stone, is the first unlit lantern you have been moving toward all this time.

Surprisingly, you don't sprint over to it howling with victory. Instead, you take slow step after slow step, approaching this ancient vessel with reverence and keeping watch over the raw flame of your torch. When you arrive, you put your hand on the outer bowl and feel the ice-cold metal singing under your skin.

For a moment you worry that your torch flame won't be strong enough to light this lantern. In response, the flame you carry roars upward as if to argue.

You lower your torch into the center of the bowl and when the fire meets the thick liquid there, the lantern bursts to life. You shield your eyes with your free hand and jump backward in the wake of the intense heat. The flame grows high and wide, reminding you of a bonfire. You move a safe distance away, finding a spot to sit and look out at the night sky and the dark ground below you.

This is a milestone moment on your journey. You have overcome countless challenges and Static to get here and you take some time to admire your progress knowing that this lantern is not only a victory for you but that the light of this beacon will help guide the way for others who have yet to start their own climb. Seeing this light on the mountain, for someone who is at the bottom and not sure they can make it, will be the assurance that they are not alone. And by staying on the path, they will find lanterns of their own to light.

CHAPTER 10

Your Lantern Checklist

By Erin

At this point you know everything you need to know to take you on the journey from choosing a Lantern to lighting it. If you have read this far and practiced the exercises here and in the Superabound Collective at *www.beSuperabound.com/collective*, you are already well on your way.

The following is a quick review that you can use and return to as you move toward your Lantern. Think of this as a guide to help you easily locate the tools you need anytime you require them.

Your Lantern Checklist:

☐ You have a clear Lantern (a.k.a. a Vision-aligned objective) you feel intrinsically motivated to reach.
   • Review chapter 4 to clarify your lantern.

☐ You know the dangers of the Goal Swamp and how to spot them before you fall in.
   • Review the trouble with goals in chapter 3.

☐ You understand the Progress Formula and the role of Vision in helping you light your Lantern.
   • Review the Progress Formula and Vision in chapters 5 and 6.

☐ You have a regular practice to help you H.E.A.L. Static and overcome Challenges with the 5Rs.
   • Review chapter 7 and chapter 8 to devise a strategy to support your inner and outer progress.

☐ You are taking excellent care of your inner fire via the Tending Triad.
   • Review the Tending Triad in chapter 9.

When You Get Stuck

If you practice your Superabound tools regularly, you will start to make progress toward your next Lantern. But there will be times when you feel stuck. One of my clients was applying for her dream job and spent three weeks putting together an application she felt good about. Her Lantern was to submit her application and she had not only the Challenges of meeting the technical requirements of the position, which took crossing some major terrain, but she also had plenty of Static to H.E.A.L.

During this process she went toe-to-toe with ancient beliefs that were holding her back about her worth and her ability to act as a leader. A few days before she was about to light her Lantern and apply, she got word from the company that they were implementing a hiring freeze.

Upon hearing this, my client told me she felt like a failure because, although she got close, she couldn't officially light her Lantern and apply for the job she wanted. But as we explored her journey up the mountain to get this far, we realized that the accomplishment was never about hitting send on her application package, it was about who she had to become to get to this moment. And we revealed that while the Lantern she was moving toward might have been fulfilling to light if she could have, it was always just a step on the path toward her Vision.

When you have moments like this, where the Lantern you were meters away from suddenly disappears, remember you are not stuck. You have to lean on your personal Tending Triad a bit more in those moments. You might even need to grieve. But once you have, return to your Superabound Vision, and get on another path toward a new aligned Lantern.

Your mountain has plenty of trails for you and many possible Lanterns you could light on the way to the summit. Join us inside the Superabound Collective at *beSuperabound.com/collective* and we will help you find them.

The Peak at Sunrise

You pause and take a deep breath and with one last tender burst of energy you maneuver around the final rock on your path, stepping up and onto the peak of the mountain. But before gazing out, you turn to look down at the journey you have had.

Each lantern you have lit on the mountain to get here shines like a firefly in the darkness. You smile to yourself at how small they seem from this height all the while knowing that each one was a microcosm of your bigger Vision, helping you to trust that you were on the path to the peak no matter how far away it seemed at times.

Very few people could ever hope to understand how choosing to climb this mountain has shaped your life, because very few people dare to commit so fully to their Superabound Vision. But you are one of the few, and in this moment you feel grateful to yourself and to the unseen forces that have been your training partners along the way.

The Static you faced was like having bowling balls in your backpack at times, not particularly helpful but, once seen and released, gave you room for more important resources.

The Challenges you had to navigate—such as which path to take and how to move as the weather and terrain changed—helped you to become resilient and confident in your ability to keep moving up the mountain, resting when needed.

You finally set down the torch in your hand, your constant companion and the outward expression of your inner flame. You know you would have been lost and wandering in the dark if not for this light.

And now here you are, standing at the top of a lifetime of living your Vision. There is no lantern here to light, so you sit down and watch the stars fade as the sky grows pale. The sun rises on the horizon and as the first beams warm your face, you feel a deep peace and contentment wash over you. You exhale and smile, letting your shoulders relax.

As the sun slowly illuminates the peak, you know without a doubt that you have led a visionary life and leave the world knowing this mountain can be climbed.

ACKNOWLEDGMENTS

This book is the product of years of coaching work with our private clients and certification students. We could not have written this book without the willingness of this incredible group of individuals who trusted us with their stories, their businesses, and their own Static. To our clients and students, thank you for showing up for your own Vision week after week; we are honored to be your coaches.

To our families: John and Julie Aquin, Michael, Virginia, Jon and Tim Haase (belated) and Julie Trafford (belated), thank you for a lifetime of love and support. We bring you with us in everything we do.

Writing a book with your partner is not for the faint of heart, so we also have to thank our kids for all the excitement and inspiration to "hurry up and finish writing so we can get back to having fun." Julian and Audrey Aquin-Haase, we can't begin to express how much we love you and hope that as you grow, this book will be a guide as you light your own Lanterns. To our Hamilton crew: Annette, Dave, Donna, Tim, Brit, Dan, Erin, Jill, John, Joe, and Katie, thanks for all the parties and good times that helped get us through this process.

We thank our friends Bev Aron, Katrina Ubell, Jenny Chammas and Lindsay Poelman for cheering us on (and coaching Erin through her own Static). Our book coach David Meerman Scott for the encouragement and insights along the way. Our awesome team at Advantage Books: Katie Smith, Ezra Byer, Matthew Morse, Harper Tucker, KJ Grow, Jenna Panzella, and many others behind the scenes, you made this book sparkle beyond what we had imagined. Thank you to the design team at Apricot: Neil and Ciele, for turning our ideas into visuals we love and to Jessi McConnell for being the most fun photographer to work with. Thanks to Steve's piano teacher, Liz Hill, who showed him the power of belief in overcoming challenges, and coach Aaron Jacobs whose questions and presence helped him ascend actual mountains.

Thanks to our teachers, friends and mentors on the path for keeping us connected with awe, gratitude, curiosity, and humor: Christopher Penczak, Amy Edelstein, Jeff Carreira, Sam Rosen, Carter Phipps, Ellen Daly, Craig Hamilton, Sarah Peyton, Bonnie Badenoch, Joel Pitney, Laura Pitney, Diane Bensel, Kenzo An, Aterah Nusrat, Morgan Dix, Steve Deckert, Caitlin Deckert, Justin Readman, Ron McLester, Cristen Brown, Collin Brown, and countless others. Your ripples of joy and presence lift us in ways you may never know.

Thank you to the rock stars who generously shared their stories for this book: Lenore Johnson, Shannin Williams, Nick Pope, Ellen Daly, and Mike Caronna.

ABOUT THE AUTHORS

Erin Aquin & Steve Haase are partners in all things life and business. They live to help people realize the life the Universe is dreaming for them and have worked with hundreds of business owners around the world to create vision-aligned companies through their work at Superabound Coaching. They live outside Waterloo, Ontario, with their two young children and are avid meditators, board game nerds, and world travelers.

CONTACT PAGE

We love helping people realize the life the Universe is dreaming for them. If you're ready to superabound in your own life, we'd love to connect. There are many paths to lighting your next Lantern and we'll help you find the right one for you and your business. Reach out to our team at hello@besuperabound.com to get started.

We have a whole world of resources for you, from helping you grow your lean team with our podcast, to having fun and sharing big ideas on Instagram. Keep learning at *www.beSuperabound.com/collective.*

Milton Keynes UK
Ingram Content Group UK Ltd.
UKHW012329240624
444664UK00012B/113/J